# Guide to Oracle® Sales Cloud Integration

Glenn C. Johnson

ISBN: 069285522X
ISBN-13: 978-0692855225 (Magic Press)

# DEDICATION

This book is dedicated to the memory of a dear friend Terry Read and my friends without homes who were served by Terry and his wife Linda Read.

# CONTENTS

# ACKNOWLEDGMENTS

I wish to acknowledge and thank the independent software vendors that are the subject of this book: Oracle publishes **Oracle CX Cloud** and **Oracle Sales Cloud**. Magic Software publishes **Magic xpi Integration Platform**. Publication of a book about software is not possible without the generous permission of these companies. I want to thank Eyal Karny, Lori McCartin, Brian Pitoniak, Izhar Fuentes, Sherrie Fry, Don White, Ted Brennan, Ryan Beck, Cheryl Slinkard, Mark Shteinberg, Stephanie Myara, Angela Burton, Sandra Ramirez, Avi Wolf, Or Gat, Eyal Rozenberg, Yuval Asheri, Udi Ertel, Arik Kilman, Guy Bernstein and countless other colleagues at Magic Software for their patience and encouragement.

# ABOUT THIS GUIDE

This book is a reference work for Oracle Sales Cloud integration, interfaces and connectivity using Magic xpi Integration Platform. By reading this book you should gain a thorough understanding of the Representational State Transfer (REST) API functions in Oracle Sales Cloud and how they can be used in the Magic xpi Integration Platform published by Magic Software.

The first two chapters of the book cover the overall capabilities of the Oracle Customer Experience Cloud, known as the Oracle CX Cloud for short (Chapter One) and the Oracle Sales Cloud (Chapter Two). In **Unit One: Oracle Sales Cloud API Resources**, we explore the ability of Magic xpi Integration Platform to manipulate the Oracle Sales Cloud REST API. Each chapter in this unit examines a particular set of Oracle Sales Cloud API calls and examines their functionality. Chapters cover: Leads, Households, Accounts, Contacts, Opportunities, Forecasts and Orders, Activities, Products, Partners, Partner Programs, Partner Program Enrollments and Benefits, Deal Registrations, Sales Management Functions, Sales Territories, Service Requests, Payments and Paysheets and Resources and Queues. In **Unit Two: Magic xpi Integration Platform**, we will investigate the detailed workings of the Magic xpi Integration Platform. We will explore chapters on Use Case Scenarios, Magic xpi Studio, Magic xpi Monitor, and Magic xpi Integration Platform Server.

An index has been provided for ease in finding specific API resources by name as well as other material not listed in the table of contents.

This **Guide to Oracle® Sales Cloud Integration** is intended as the first book in the CLOUD INTEGRATION SERIES by Magic Press.

# 1 ORACLE CX CLOUD INTEGRATION OVERVIEW

 The **Oracle Customer Experience (CX) Cloud** is comprised of five main Oracle Cloud offerings: Oracle Marketing Cloud; Oracle Sales Cloud; Oracle Service Cloud; Oracle Field Service Cloud; Oracle Configure, Price, and Quote Cloud; Oracle Commerce Cloud. Let's begin by looking at a high level at how **Magic xpi Integration Platform** provides **Oracle CX Cloud** integration. While Oracle CX cloud provides a full set of APIs, an integration platform greatly simplifies the management of those APIs and the connections between them and your other cloud and on-premise enterprise systems.

**Oracle Marketing Cloud Integration.** Magic xpi provides Oracle Marketing Cloud Integration for Oracle Eloqua in the Cloud. Magic xpi automates Oracle Eloqua REST APIs that enable you to extend the functionality of the Oracle Eloqua product, build Apps, and perform high volume data transfers. In addition, Magic xpi can automate API integration to Oracle Content Marketing, Oracle Data Management Platform, Oracle Responsys, Oracle Social Relationship Management, Oracle Maxymiser and Oracle Data as a Service for Customer Intelligence.

**Oracle Sales Cloud Integration.** Magic xpi can integrate Oracle Sales Cloud using REST and SOAP Web Services as well as file loader approaches. Magic xpi automates the use of Oracle Sales Cloud APIs and intermediates with other on-premise enterprise and cloud applications (both Oracle and non-Oracle).

**Oracle Service Cloud Integration.** Businesses use Oracle Service Cloud to improve CX and NPS by developing lasting and profitable relationships with unified web, social, and contact center experiences. Magic xpi can automate Oracle Service Cloud business processes and integrate data using REST, SOAP, .Net and JavaScript APIs for Oracle Service Cloud. The benefit of an automated approach using Magic xpi lies in the simplified approach to data mapping, transformation, business logic, and real-time event management and scheduling.

**Oracle Field Service Cloud Integration.** Oracle Field Service Cloud is built on time-based, self-learning, and predictive technology, allowing modern field service organizations to solve business problems while evolving your field service organization. Magic xpi automates Oracle Field Service REST APIs to access data stored in Field Service Cloud and orchestrate business processes with other systems. Magic xpi connects other Oracle Cloud applications as well as external systems in the cloud or on-premise.

**Oracle CPQ Cloud.** The Oracle Configure, Price, and Quote Cloud (Oracle CPQ Cloud) is designed to streamline end-to-end opportunity-to-quote-to-order processes such as product selection, configuration, pricing, quoting, ordering, and approval workflows. Magic xpi automates the data integration and process orchestration of Oracle CPQ Cloud services via REST APIs.

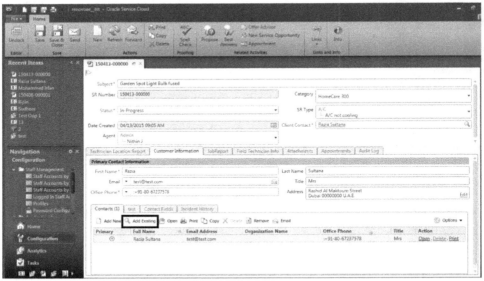

**Figure 1a.** Oracle CPQ Cloud.

**Oracle Commerce Cloud.** The Oracle Commerce Cloud Service provides a service platform upon which to build a flexible, feature-rich storefront and go to market quickly with Oracle Cloud technology and infrastructure. Magic xpi can automate Oracle Commerce Cloud payment gateway integration, shipping services, 3PL, order management systems,

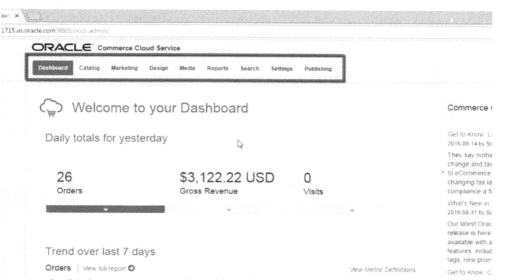

web checkout systems, and a wide variety of cloud and on-premise systems including ERP, CRM, PLM, SCM and others.

**Figure 1b.** Oracle Commerce Cloud.

Leveraging Magic xpi Integration Platform to integrate Oracle CX Cloud requires about 5 days of training. Although self-paced materials are available, the best approach is with a classroom instructor.

**Oracle Marketing Cloud.** Oracle offers the Oracle Eloqua Marketing Cloud Service as part of the Oracle Marketing Cloud in the Oracle CX Cloud. Oracle Eloqua Marketing Cloud Service offers capabilities for Web Marketing, Lead Management, Marketing Ops, Marketing Measurement, Targeting, Sales Enablement and Integration.

In this discussion of Oracle CX Cloud, we will identify how Magic xpi Integration Platform can access the Data Integration related REST APIs from the Oracle Cloud Marketing Service to extend the functionality of the product and perform high volume data transfers. Oracle Eloqua Marketing Cloud Service offers a 1.0 and a 2.0 API. Let's first explore the 1.0 API capabilities for Data Integration.

**Account Integration.** In Eloqua, an account, also known as a company, is a data entity that contains explicit data around a customer account or prospective account in the Eloqua database. Along with contacts, accounts are used as building blocks for segments, and are central to account-based marketing. Magic xpi can post (create), delete, put (update), and get Eloqua Accounts in the Oracle Marketing Cloud.

**Contact Integration.** In Eloqua, a contact is a data entity that contains the explicit data around an individual person in the database. Contacts (and associated accounts) are used as the primary building blocks for segments. Contact information can be derived from email responses or form submissions, from website visits, event registrations or via external (non-Eloqua) activities. Magic xpi can post (create), delete, put (update), and get Eloqua Contacts in the Oracle Marketing Cloud.

**Figure 1c.** Oracle Eloqua Cloud user interface.

**Contact Fields Integration.** In Eloqua, a contact field is a property associated with a contact. A contact field is populated with specific information such as First Name, City, Email, Company, and so on. You may define any additional custom fields that you require to track contacts. Magic xpi can post (create), delete, put (update), and get Eloqua Contact Fields in the Oracle Marketing Cloud.

**Contact List Integration.** In Eloqua, a Contact List contains a specific list of custom contacts. Lists contain specific named contacts regardless of any criteria. In this sense, they are different from filters which are used to build segments based on the filter criteria. Magic xpi can post (create), delete, put (update), and get Eloqua Contact Lists in the Oracle Marketing Cloud.

**Segment Integration.** In Eloqua, Segments are groups of contacts that are generated based on filter criteria and contact lists. Segments can filter contacts based on criteria like whether or not they receive a newspaper, or whether or not they visited a landing page. Magic xpi can post (create), delete, put (update), and get Eloqua Segments in the Oracle Marketing Cloud.

**Custom Objects and Data Integration.** In Eloqua, a custom object contains custom records beyond the standard contact and account records. Magic xpi can post (create), delete, put (update), and get Eloqua Custom Objects and post (create), and get Custom Object Data in the Oracle Marketing Cloud.

**User Integration.** Eloqua application users and user information can be retrieved and updated automatically. Magic xpi can put (update), and get Eloqua Users and User Information in the Oracle Marketing Cloud. This is used for obtaining information such as the user's time zone.

**Forms Integration and Form Data Integration.** Eloqua forms provide an interactive way for customers and prospects to provide input, data and give permission such as opting into a campaign or subscribing to a list. By filling in their information and submitting the form, email recipients or landing page visitors are "opting in" to your marketing campaign (this should be clearly stated in the text associated with the form). Forms also collect information about visitors when they want to access demos, whitepapers, and other marketing content. Magic xpi can post (create), delete, put (update), and get Eloqua Forms. Magic xpi can also post (create), and get Form Data for a specified form in the Oracle Marketing Cloud.

**Activities Integration.** Eloqua keeps track of the activities of individual contacts. The types of activities tracked are: emailOpen, emailSend, emailClickThrough, emailSubscribe, emailUnsubscribe, formSubmit, webVisit, or campaignMembership. Using the Eloqua REST API, Magic xpi can only get Eloqua Activities according to selected criteria.

Interacting with the data of Oracle Marketing Cloud offers possibilities for integration to other applications such as CRM, specialized marketing applications, etc. Eloqua, for example, is a marketing automation platform but does not offer extensive social media features. Some organizations may want to utilize Oracle Marketing Cloud/Eloqua for outbound email marketing campaigns but use other marketing platforms for online advertising, inbound marketing and social media marketing. The availability of the REST APIs makes it possible to pursue such integration and still reap the benefits of Oracle Eloqua Marketing Cloud.

**Process Integration.** Magic xpi Integration Platform can also access the Process Integration related REST APIs from the Oracle Cloud Marketing Service to extend the functionality of the product and perform high volume data transfers. Oracle Eloqua Marketing Cloud Service offers a

1.0 and a 2.0 API. In this post we will explore the 1.0 API capabilities for Process Integration.

For our purposes, the process related API capabilities relate to Emails, Landing Pages, Microsites and their components such as Content Sections, Images and Option Lists.

**Email Integration.** In Eloqua, the REST API allows Magic xpi to create HTML emails. HTML Emails contain the various Content Segments, Forms, Images, Links, FieldMerges, HTML and other information needed to comprise an email.

**Email Groups Integration.** Email Groups are used to control default settings for similar types of emails. For instance, you can set the default header, footer, subscription landing page, and unsubscribe landing page for a set of email newsletters. Then your contacts can subscribe or unsubscribe at the group level to simplify subscription management. As an administrator, you can add or delete groups as required to control email subscriptions. Magic xpi can post (create), delete, put (update), and get Eloqua Email Groups in the Oracle Marketing Cloud.

**Email Header and Footer Integration.** Email headers are used to customize the look and feel of the top of your email while Email footers are used to customize the look and feel of the bottom of your email. Headers and footers can be used in your emails for branding purposes (your company's logo), to provide a "call to action" such as links to other (external) resources, or to display the link for a contact to view the email in a browser. Email headers and footers are automatically added to your email after selecting and saving the email group to which it belongs, but you can also select a different header or footer on a per-email basis from the email header chooser. Magic xpi can post (create), delete, put (update), and get Eloqua Email Headers and Footers in the Oracle Marketing Cloud.

**Email Folders Integration.** Email folders organize the way email assets are organized within the Eloqua application user interface. Magic xpi can post (create), delete, put (update), and get Eloqua Email Folders in the Oracle Marketing Cloud.

**Landing Page Integration.** In Eloqua, a Landing Page is an HTML web page displayed most often as the starting point of a particular campaign. The Landing Page is served by your web server and viewed inside a prospect or customers web browser. Landing pages can contain various Content Segments, Forms, Images, Links, FieldMerges, HTML and other matter. Magic xpi can post (create), delete, put (update), and get Eloqua Landing Pages in the Oracle Marketing Cloud.

**Microsite Integration.** A microsite is a small Eloqua website covering a specific campaign, product, or keyword. The purpose is to provide detailed marketing information and response opportunities (Calls to Action). Every landing page in Eloqua requires a microsite. Magic xpi can post (create), delete, put (update), and get Eloqua Microsites in the Oracle Marketing Cloud.

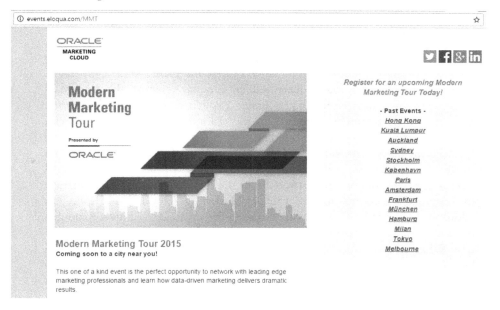

**Figure 1d.** Oracle Marketing Cloud microsite.

**Dynamic Content Integration.** In Eloqua, Content sections are used to create custom dynamic content to use inside assets such as emails and landing pages. Magic xpi can post (create), delete, put (update), and get Eloqua Content sections in the Oracle Marketing Cloud.

**Image Integration.** In Eloqua, Image assets are used in places such as emails or landing pages. Image file types supported include gif, jpg, jpeg, pgn, and svg. Magic xpi can post (create), delete, put (update), and get Eloqua Images in the Oracle Marketing Cloud.

**Option Lists Integration.** Option lists in Eloqua are used in either forms, landing pages or microsites. They are drop down lists provided for user interaction. For example, a form could have a drop down list for Color that offered the options of Autumn Gold, Burnt Sienna, Aquamarine and Red. Magic xpi can post (create), delete, put (update), and get Eloqua Option Lists in the Oracle Marketing Cloud.

**REST API 2.0.** Magic xpi Integration Platform can access the extended capabilities of the Oracle Eloqua Marketing Cloud REST API 2.0 for the same basic structures of Data Integration and Process Integration handled by the REST API 1.0.

The Magic xpi Integration Platform can access the Oracle Eloqua

Marketing Cloud REST API 2.0 covers additional capabilities for Accounts, Contacts, Custom Objects, and Custom Object Data. In addition, the 2.0 API introduces capabilities for Account Groups, Campaigns, Email Deployment, External Activities, External Assets, External Asset Types, Visitors, and Visitor Profile Fields.

Adding to the capabilities of the Eloqua Cloud Marketing API 1.0, the 2.0 API provides extended and enhanced capabilities for:

**Accounts.** As previously described, an Eloqua Account, also known as a company, is a data entity that contains explicit data around a customer account or prospective account in the Eloqua database. Along with contacts, accounts are used as building blocks for segments, and are central to account-based marketing. Magic xpi can post (create), delete, put (update), and get Eloqua Accounts in the Oracle Marketing Cloud (API 1.0). Magic xpi can get information about the Account Group memberships of specified Accounts in the Oracle Marketing Cloud (API 2.0). In addition, Magic xpi can post search results for up to 200 Eloqua Accounts by search id. The depth of the information may be complete or partial (API 2.0). While it may seem counter-intuitive that a POST is used to retrieve a list of accounts, one should keep in mind that the API is essentially getting the list of accounts and then posting the search results, therefore this API functionality is ultimately classified as a POST activity.

**Contacts.** As previously described, an Eloqua Contact is a data entity that contains the explicit data around an individual person in the database. Contacts (and associated accounts) are used as the primary building blocks for segments. Contact information can be derived from email responses or form submissions, from website visits, event registrations or via external (non-Eloqua) activities. Magic xpi can post (create), delete, put (update), and get Eloqua Contacts in the Oracle Marketing Cloud (API 1.0). Magic xpi can get a list of the Contact Lists that a specified Contact belongs to (API 2.0). In addition, Magic xpi can post search results for up to 200 Eloqua Contacts by search id. The depth of the information may be complete or partial (API 2.0). For the same reasons discussed above in regards to accounts, the search results activity are regarded as a POST rther than a GET.

**Custom Objects and Custom Object Data.** As previously stated, an Eloqua Custom Object contains custom records beyond the standard contact and account records. Magic xpi can post (create), delete, put (update), and get Eloqua Custom Objects and post (create), and get Custom Object Data in the Oracle Marketing Cloud (API 1.0). With the 2.0 API, Magic xpi can also manage Custom Objects permissions and Custom Object Data permissions in Oracle Eloqua Marketing Cloud as well as delete and update Custom Object Data (with permissions) (API 2.0).

While these capabilities discussed here are essentially enhancements to the capabilities offered Magic xpi Integration Platform via the Oracle Eloqua Marketing Cloud API 1.0, in our next entry we will explore enhanced capabilities for Account Groups, Campaigns, Email Deployment, External Activities, External Assets, External Asset Types, Visitors, and Visitor Profile Fields.

While all of these API capabilities are useful, the lack of campaign management in the API 1.0 was particularly difficult. In Eloqua, campaigns are central to the management of marketing processes and constitute a fundamental element of workflow and activity for the marketing department using Eloqua Marketing Cloud.

We have been particularly eager to see these capabilities added to the REST API 2.0 because marketing Campaigns are at the center of the Eloqua application. Indeed, Eloqua campaigns are comprised of the various different elements that we have already discussed such as segments, emails, landing pages, microsites, contacts, accounts, etc.) that are used to perform a variety of functions. Because you can combine the different elements in a number of ways to customize your campaign flow, the campaign capabilities of the Eloqua Marketing Cloud REST API 2.0 will prove to be central to business process orchestration in the Oracle Eloqua Marketing Cloud.

**Figure 1e.** Oracle Content Marketing.

**Oracle Content Marketing.** Oracle Content Marketing is designed to fill the need for organizations to create customized content for specific individuals as needed and delivered through the preferred communication channel. Oracle Content Marketing manages the use of varied types of content contributors such as customers, employees and contractors. This SaaS app manages the planning and collaboration process to create content across the planning, production, and delivery phase for multi- persona and multi-channel content creation across the customer lifecycle.

As a software-as-a-Service (SaaS) app, Oracle Content Marketing provides online marketers a central location to plan, produce, publish, and promote a wide variety of content. Aside from the ability for users to access the application via the Web, Magic xpi can automate Oracle Content Marketing via a set of application programming interfaces (APIs) which can be used to integrate data and orchestrate event-driven processes.

Magic xpi Integration Platform automates Oracle Content Marketing in the cloud using the provided APIs, intermediates connections and communications with third-party systems and orchestrates smooth running end-to-end business processes in a real-time event architecture.

**Analytics Pageviews.** Tracking pixels are little 1x1 pixel transparent images that allow you to keep track of how many users visit you're a webpage or see a piece of content. The one-pixel image solves an intrinsic problem for web-based analytics apps (like Google Analytics) when working in the HTTP Protocol--how to transfer (web metrics) data from the client to the server. In our present discussion, Magic xpi Integration Platform is able to track content views using the Analytics Pageview API.

**Workflow Stages.** In Oracle Content Marketing, Workflow Stages are used to define steps that all Content Assets should take. Workflow Stages are grouped by before approval and after approval stages. At the instant a Content Asset has passed the final pre-approval stage, Oracle Content Marketing regards it as approved. OCM will publish it when the publication date arrives. There are three pre-defined system Workflow Stages within OCM: "Idea", "Draft", and "Complete". Magic xpi automates the create (POST), read (GET), update (PUT), and delete (DELETE) of Workflow Stages.

**Workflow Tasks.** Workflow Tasks are the specific tasks that must be completed within a Workflow Stage. These are the key components of the OCM Workflow system. Magic xpi can automate the OCM system to List Workflow Tasks, Get Workflow Tasks, Update Workflow Tasks, Create Workflow Tasks and Delete Workflow Tasks.

**Workflows.** Workflow Tasks and Workflow Stages are components of a Workflow. In fact, Workflows are said to be a collection of Workflow Tasks which are described by or contained within a Workflow Stage. By applying a Content Asset to a Workflow, the content process is managed. Multiple Workflows may be applied to a Content Asset to provide it with a complex set of Stages and Tasks.

Another thing to keep in mind about Workflows is that they can be designated to a Content Asset on a case-by-case basis or can be systematically applied to Content Assets based upon Workflow rules in the Workflow. The groups of Content Assets designated to a w Workflow can be passed on various Content Types, Publishers, Categories, or Authors. Universal Workflows can also be designated for all Content Assets.

Magic xpi can automatically get a list of Workflows, get a particular Workflow, create a Workflow, activate or deactivate a Workflow, or modify an existing Workflow.

**Content Stages.** The Content Stages in Oracle Content Marketing are used to measure the degree of engagement with the content. An engagement stage such as "awareness" or "consideration" can be tagged to a Content Asset and Workflow stage via the Content Stages Api. Magic xpi can perform basic CRUD operations on an Oracle Content Marketing app's Content Stages.

**Content Workflows.** In Oracle Content Marketing, the term Content Workflow designates the tagging of a Workflow to a Content Asset. Magic xpi can automatically get a list of Workflows, get a particular Workflow, create a Workflow, activate or deactivate a Workflow, or modify an existing Workflow. Magic xpi can automatically Get All Workflows, Get a Specific Workflow, List Workflows on a Content Asset, Modify an Existing Workflow, Create a Workflow or Activate/Deactivate a Workflow on a Content Asset.

**Content Tasks.** In Oracle Content Marketing, a Content Task is a Task that is tagged to a Content Asset. "Similar to Content Stages, Content Tasks are created as copies of Workflow Tasks at the time of a Content Asset create or edit." A one-off Content Task may also be created for a specific Content Asset.

Magic xpi can automate these Content Task processes: Update Content Task Completion, List Content Tasks, Get a Content Task, Create a Content Task, Update a Content Task, Delete a Content Task, List the Authenticated Users Current Tasks, and List All of the Authenticated Users Tasks.

**External Connection Publisher.** Magic xpi can automate Oracle Content Marketing notifications of external applications. In Oracle Content Marketing, External Connection Publishers allow Magic xpi to receive "push" events every time a content asset is changed and Magic xpi can then manage notifications to other applications, people or processes. These events are handled as HTTP POST requests to a designated callback URL. The response payload will return the current state of the content asset, its contents and metadata.

In summary, Magic xpi Integration Platform provides the needed automation capabilities for Oracle Content Marketing within the Oracle Marketing Cloud.

**Oracle Commerce Integration.** The challenge of integrating an eCommerce platform with Oracle Sales Cloud is not to be taken lightly. While eCommerce platforms may seem like mere websites, they are powered by very complex content management and transaction systems that affect core business processes: namely orders which are also a key concern of any CRM system.

**Figure 1f.** Oracle Cloud Commerce Webhook API setup.

**Market Forces Drive Integration.** Many of the companies that are using Oracle Sales Cloud are looking to eCommerce platforms like Oracle Commerce Platform, Magento, IBM WebSphere Commerce, Shopatron and others to provide a web transaction front-end for their consumer customers and business channel partners. And why not? According to eMarketer, non-travel eCommerce sales are nearing $300 billion in 2014 and will likely reach $434 billion by 2017. One of the hottest areas of eCommerce is mobile commerce, sometimes called mCommerce. Studies show nearly half of all mobile users have purchased a digital product online, one-in- four have bought clothing, and one-in five have purchased travel, entertainment and physical products and most of these purchases have been done using credit and debit cards.

**Integration Methods.** In the case of JD Edwards integration with Oracle Commerce Platform (formerly Oracle ATG Web Commerce), the challenge of integration is significant but certainly not insurmountable. The Oracle Commerce Platform API allows for interaction via a REST MVC Server that supports REST Web Services. Other options for integration include SOAP wrapped xml Web Services and Java Message Service (JMS). Magic xpi Integration Platform facilitates the orchestration, mediation and transformation of data and processes between Oracle Commerce Platform integration services and Oracle JD Edwards Business Functions (BSFN) and flat files (z-files) using any of these three methods (REST, SOAP or JMS).

**Scalability for Commerce.** The extreme scalability of Magic xpi's in-memory data grid is particularly well-suited to the high volume "Big Data" challenges likely with Oracle Commerce Platform clients. Much has been written about the fact that successful eCommerce websites must be efficiently architected for potentially high amounts of traffic. In particular, seasonal spikes in demand for holiday seasons can cause websites to suffer poor performance, delays, errors in processing up to and including total system failure. Nobody wants to find out their eCommerce integration broke on Black Friday or Cyber Monday, because as we all know that can lead to "Pink Slip Tuesday." However, many forget to evaluate integration layers for scalability and can find that the synchronization and real-time inquiries and processes that need to take place between the eCommerce platform, the ERP system (and perhaps other key systems such as Agile PLM) are not adequately scalable.

Magic xpi also helps with the needed security for eCommerce integration. With a broad range of cybersecurity measures such as encryption and decryption, operation behind the firewall, and complete traceability, the integration middleware is assured of passing the security audit too.

# 2 ORACLE SALES CLOUD INTEGRATION OVERVIEW

If you want to improve customer experience in the **Oracle Cloud**, you use **Oracle CX Cloud**. That's what you do. If you want to improve sales in your company, you do a better job of managing sales, that's what you do.

Oracle Sales Cloud is a cloud-based Software-as-a-Service or SaaS solution that manages sales force automation tasks for a business or organization on an end-to-end basis in the cloud. Sitting alongside other members of the Oracle CX Cloud, the platform is focused on selling activities and sales management. The other Oracle CX Cloud components are: Oracle Marketing Cloud; Oracle Sales Cloud; Oracle Service Cloud; Oracle Field Service Cloud; Oracle Configure, Price, and Quote Cloud; Oracle Commerce Cloud.

The Guide to Oracle® Sales Cloud Integration is a reference work describing the API resources of the Oracle Sales Cloud REST API and Magic xpi Integration Platform automation of integration processes through the REST API.

Magic xpi Integration Platform is a very smart, efficient tool and platform that allows you to create any cloud-to-cloud, cloud-to-on=premise (hybrid), or on-premise-to-on-premise enterprise software or SaaS integration. The drag, drop and configure approach is ideal for a business analyst or developer in an IT department that is seeking a no-code approach to the complex world of cloud, SaaS and application integration. It neither oversimplifies or over complicates the business of integration by providing a balanced visual approach with powerful data mappers and expression editors that give you the power to define how your applications should integrate.

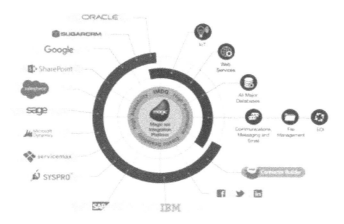

**Figure 2.** Illustrator's Depiction of Magic xpi Integration Platform Architecture. (Image Courtesy: Magic Software Enterprises, Ltd. Copyright 2016. All Rights Reserved).

Magic xpi consumes REST APIs, SOAP APIs and can interact with data loaders in the various Oracle Cloud APIs or third party Cloud APIs as needed. In addition, Magic xpi Integration Platform connects with on-premise applications already in your portfolio to give your business analyst or developer the ability to define the integration processes flows in your integration project. Every business has unique requirements and settings and yet you do not want to reinvent all the connectivity and brokering of communications needed to be fully integrated. Even Oracle Cloud applications require some integration to one another. You need a no-code tool to do that. Magic xpi provides the right balance between pre-built adapters that connect automatically to your applications and powerful data mapping that allows you to describe and define "what" to do once connections are established. The "what" is always different depending on your needs and requirements. Magic does eliminate the need for you to decide on your business processes, but it does greatly simplify how you can do it yourself (DIY). As a DIY integrator, you save your business time and money in integration effort and have an easy-to-maintain integration solution that doesn't break every time you upgrade an app.

To Integrate Oracle Sales Cloud using Magic xpi Integration Platform you use the Magic xpi Studio to set up your project, business processes and specific integration flows (see Chapter 21). Once your project and its integration flows are designed, you'll need to decide how to deploy it on-premise or in the cloud. How much redundancy and performance do you need for your project? How will you manage the In Memory Data Grid capabilities? These settings are configured when you setup the Magic xpi Server (see Chapter 23). Once the project is running, you can use the Magic Monitor (see Chapter 22) to see how well the integration processes are performing and gain visibility to dashboard and log views of the Operational Data Store.

Before getting into the details of the Magic xpi Integration Platform, UNIT ONE describes in detail the integration abilities of Magic xpi made possible by the Oracle Sales Cloud REST API (See Chapters 3-19). By learning these API capabilities at a high level, you will understand the building blocks of your integration project. As you develop true expertise in the capabilities, your ability manage an integration project successfully is greatly enhanced.

# UNIT ONE: ORACLE SALES CLOUD API RESOURCES

# 3 INTEGRATION WITH ORACLE SALES CLOUD SALES LEADS

Dealing with sales leads is an integral part of any Customer Relationship Management system. In the Oracle Customer Experience Cloud, better known as the Oracle CX Cloud, Oracle Sales Cloud is the core of the CRM system capabilities that can deal with sales leads. Magic xpi Integration Platform is used to automate information integration and data processes for Oracle Sales Cloud including Oracle Sales Cloud Sales Leads business objects.

| Oracle Sales Cloud REST API: Sales Lead Resources |
| --- |
| Sales Leads |
| Notes |
| Opportunities |
| Product Groups |
| Products |
| Sales Lead Contacts |
| Sales Lead Products |
| Sales Lead Resources |
| Table 3:Sales Lead Resources |

**Sales Leads.** In Oracle Sales Cloud, a sales lead resource is used to view, create, or modify a lead. A lead is a transaction record created when a party has expressed an interest in a product or service. It represents a selling opportunity. Magic xpi can automate the creation (POST), deletion (DELETE), listing (GET), retrieval (GET), and updating (PATCH) of a

18

Sales Lead. Magic xpi can also use the POST function for a sales lead to assign leads and convert leads.

**Assigning Leads.** Magic xpi can automate the assignment of Sales Leads in Oracle Sales Cloud based on external triggers, data and processes. Magic xpi runs the assignment in Oracle Sales Cloud for the passed in lead identifier and assigns either resources or territories to the lead.

**Converting Leads into Opportunities.** Magic xpi can automate the conversion of Sales Leads in Oracle Sales Cloud based on external triggers, data and processes. Magic xpi runs the conversion in Oracle Sales Cloud and converts the passed in lead identifier to an opportunity.

Magic xpi can automatically get a list (GET) or retrieve an individual opportunity (GET).

An opportunity has the following properties:

- *Account.* The account associated with the lead.
- *Currency.* The currency code associated with the opportunity revenue amount.
- *Lead Name.* Name of the lead on the opportunity that was created from the lead.
- *Lead Number.* Number of the lead that was used to create opportunity.
- *Opportunity Close Date.* Close date of the opportunity associated with the lead.
- *Opportunity ID.* The unique identifier of the opportunity that was created by converting the lead.
- *Opportunity Name.* Name of the opportunity that was created by converting the lead.
- *Opportunity Number.* Opportunity number of the opportunity associated with the lead.
- *Opportunity Status.* Status of the opportunity associated with the lead.
- *Revenue Amount.* Revenue amount of the opportunity associated with the lead.
- *Sales Stage Id.* Unique identifier of

---

**Hot Use Case: Marketo**

Marketo is one of the leading third-party marketing automation platforms on the market today. Many sales and marketing organizations that choose Oracle Sales Cloud will already have a Marketo implementation in place. Using Magic xpi Integration Platform, Oracle Sales Cloud and Marketo can easily coexist.

Marketo excels at creating landing pages, emails, marketing programs and engagement campaigns. Marketo can manage the marketing pool of leads, adding to the lead score as prospects interact with emails and Web pages. Magic xpi can synchronize the lead database in Marketo with the lead database in Oracle Sales Cloud including the lead score and other data.

the sales stage of the opportunity associated with the lead.

- *Sales Stage Name.* Name of the sales stage of the opportunity associated with the lead.
- *Win Probability.* Win probability of the opportunity associated with the lead.

**Lead Notes.** In Oracle Sales Cloud, a Lead Note resource records information such as comments, descriptive information, or special instructions related to a lead. A note is a record attached to a business object. Notes capture nonstandard information received as you do business, especially unstructured text. Magic xpi can automatically create (POST), delete (DELETE), get a list (GET), retrieve an individual note (GET), or update (PATCH) data that is pertaining to a Lead Note.

**Product Groups.** In Oracle Sales Cloud, a Product Group is a business object that contains related products. An example of a product group name is Women's Fashion and it might include all of your clothing and accessories products for women so that customers can browse through all the products in this group in your product catalog. Using Magic xpi, your business analyst may automate the creation (POST), deletion (DELETE), listing (GET), retrieval (GET), and updating (PATCH) of Product Groups. Using Magic xpi, your business analyst or developer can also automatically capture the name of the product group associated with the sales lead or opportunity.

Hot Use Case: Hubspot

Hubspot is another leading third-party marketing automation platform that also has some sales automation capabilities. As more sales and marketing organizations that choose Hubspot also choose Oracle Sales Cloud, the need for integration is increasing. Using Magic xpi Integration Platform, Oracle Sales Cloud and Hubspot can coexist without resorting to programming.

Marketo excels at inbound marketing, social campaigns and nurturing campaigns. Hubspot can manage the marketing pool of leads, adding to the lead score as prospects interact with emails, social sites and your company Web pages. Magic xpi can synchronize the lead database in Hubspot with the lead database in Oracle Sales Cloud including the lead score and other relevant marketing data.

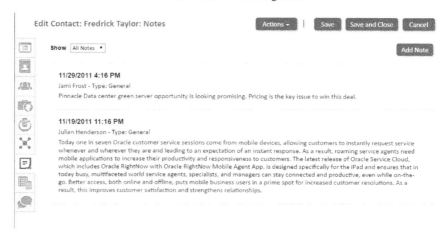

**Figure 3a.** Contact Notes shown in user interface.

In Oracle Sales Cloud, locking a product group makes it inaccessible or non editable by other users while you are making some changes. Magic xpi can use the creation (POST) function to lock a product group, publish a list of all locked product groups, or release the lock on a product group. Publishing the product group makes the changes available to the users at runtime.

**Figure 3a.** Oracle Sales Cloud User Interface.

**Products.** In Oracle Sales Cloud, the product resource is a sub resource of the lead or opportunity. Generally, it is used to view, create, or modify a product. A product is a good or service that your company wants to sell. In Oracle Sales Cloud, once you create a product, you cannot delete it. However, you can "hide" products in consuming applications by adjusting the Eligible to Sell property. Using Magic xpi, your business analyst or developer may automate the creation (POST), listing (GET), retrieval (GET), and updating (PATCH) of Products. Using Magic xpi, your business analyst or developer can also automatically capture the name of the product associated with the sales lead or opportunity.

**Sales Leads Contacts.** In Oracle Sales Cloud, the sales lead contact resource is used to capture a contact associated with the sales lead. Magic xpi can automate the creation (POST), deletion (DELETE), listing (GET), retrieval (GET), and updating (PATCH) of a Sales Lead Contact.

**Sales Leads Products.** In Oracle Sales Cloud, the sales lead products resource is used to capture a product associated with the sales lead. Magic xpi can automate the creation (POST), deletion (DELETE), listing (GET), retrieval (GET), and updating (PATCH) of a Sales Lead Product.

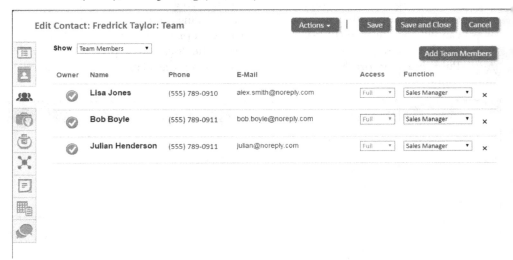

**Figure 3b.** Assigning team members as resources in the user interface

**Sales Leads Resources.** In Oracle Sales Cloud, a sales lead resource is a data object (resource) used to capture information associated with the sales lead team members associated to the lead. A lead resource is a business object that is used to represent resources who are team members that form part of the lead sales team. Magic xpi can automate the creation (POST), deletion (DELETE), listing (GET), retrieval (GET), and updating (PATCH) of Sales Lead Resources.

Magic xpi's ability to automate the handling of sales leads and opportunities in Oracle Sales Cloud and integrate them with other systems such as marketing automation, CPQ, ERP and ecommerce platforms makes it an essential tool in the integration toolkit of any IT department responsible for users of Oracle Sales Cloud.

# 4 INTEGRATION WITH ORACLE SALES CLOUD HOUSEHOLDS

 **Oracle CX Cloud** uses **Oracle Sales Cloud** as the Customer Relationship Management (**CRM**) system and it is well suited to both **B2B** and **B2C** customer relationships. In fact, Oracle Sales Cloud has a well designed data structure for management of information relating to **Households**. Integrating Household data and processes using the **Oracle Sales Cloud REST API**s allows us a significant number of automation capabilities. We will spend some time discussing the suitability of Oracle Sales Cloud for use as a Partner Relationship Management system in a B2B context when we get to *Chapter 11: Partners*. But Households are primarily relevant when your target is consumers.

| Oracle Sales Cloud REST API: Households Resources |
|---|
| Households |
| Addresses |
| Address Purposes |
| Attachments |
| Aux Classifications |
| Notes |
| Primary Addresses |
| Relationships |
| Sales Account Resources |
| Table 4:Household Resources |

Oracle Sales Cloud's household API resource is used to view, create, and update a household. In Oracle Sales Cloud, a Household is a group that has a relationship with either an account or a contact. As in similar systems, a household object includes attributes that are used to store values while creating or updating a household. Magic xpi Integration Platform can manage household data and processes in an automated fashion for the Oracle Sales Cloud user based on your business rules. In this fashion, Magic xpi can use the child resources such as addresses, relationships, addressPurposes, salesTeamMembers, and primary addresses to also manage child entities of the household object.

In Oracle Sales Cloud, comprehensive customer information can be stored in the accounts, contacts, and households objects.

An Oracle Sales Cloud user manages the data in customers and prospects to qualify accounts, contacts, and households. Customers and prospects can be organizations such as businesses or non-profits or government agencies and in these cases are stored as Accounts. Or customers and prospects can be individuals that are stored as contacts or group of individuals that are recorded as households.

You can use the comprehensive Oracle Sales Cloud accounts, contacts, and households management capabilities to create and update accounts, contacts, and households; enrich the information in accounts and contacts; maintain the relationships of accounts in account hierarchies; and even manage multiple industry classifications. In a B2B context, any organization can be an account that a salesperson sells to and can be a prospect or customer. Oracle Sales Cloud can create leads and opportunities within accounts. In the B2C context, any person can be a contact which is to say a prospect or customer. A person may also be both a customer as well as a contact of another customer.

So what is a household? A household is a group of contacts with whom you have a selling relationship. Households provide valuable segmentation and classification information about the household as a whole, as well as summary of information about the household member contacts. Household can have an average age, a number of members below age 7, and a total household income, for example. Usually all the contacts reside at the same address and have a similar set of sales relationship attributes that accounts do, such as team members, territories, and contacts.

**Households.** In Oracle Sales Cloud, a household represents a group of contacts with whom your business has a selling relationship. Magic xpi Integration Platform can be used to automate the creation (POST), deletion (DELETE), listing (GET), retrieval (GET), and updating (PATCH) of Households in Oracle Sales Cloud.

**Household Addresses.** In Oracle Sales Cloud, the household address contains an address associated to a household. Magic xpi Integration Platform can be used to automate the creation (POST), deletion

(DELETE), listing (GET), retrieval (GET), and updating (PATCH) of Household Addresses in Oracle Sales Cloud.

**Household Address Purpose.** In Oracle Sales Cloud, the purpose of an address is used to describe things such as SHIP_TO, BILL_TO, HOME_OFFICE, SHIPPING_YARD and other address purposes which are defined during setup. Magic xpi Integration Platform can be used to automate the creation (POST), deletion (DELETE), listing (GET), retrieval (GET), and updating (PATCH) of Household Address Purposes in Oracle Sales Cloud.

**Household Notes.** The Household Notes provide a means whereby a note can be associated to a Household record in Oracle Sales Cloud. Using Magic xpi Integration Platform, you can automate the creation (POST), deletion (DELETE), listing (GET), retrieval (GET), and updating (PATCH) of a Household Note. In addition to all of the relationship data and metadata, the core of a note is the NoteTxt field which is an unlimited string text field containing the actual Note text.

**Household Attachments.** In Oracle Sales Cloud, a household record may contain attachments. Using Magic xpi, your business analyst may automate the creation (POST), deletion (DELETE), listing (GET), retrieval (GET), and updating (PATCH) of Household Attachments.

**Household Aux Classifications.** In Oracle Sales Cloud, a household record may Auxiliary Classifications. Using Magic xpi, your business analyst may automate the creation (POST), deletion (DELETE), listing (GET), retrieval (GET), and updating (PATCH) of Household Aux Classifications.

**Household Primary Address.** The Household Primary Address capability built into Oracle Sales Cloud can be used by Magic xpi to read, create, and update the primary address for the location of a household. You can regard the primary address of a household as the default communication address of that household. Magic xpi can automate the creation (POST), deletion (DELETE), listing (GET), retrieval (GET), and updating (PATCH) of a Household Primary Addresses.

**Household Relationships.** Household Relationship Types are typically defined using the Setup and Maintenance area of the Oracle Sales Cloud application by an administrative user. Once defined, the Household Relationships can be listed, viewed and created for any particular household programmatically. In Oracle Sales Cloud, the Household Relationship resource includes properties that are used to store values while viewing, creating, or updating a relationship. Using Magic xpi Integration Platform, you can automate the creation (POST), listing (GET), and retrieval (GET) of a Household Relationship.

**Household Sales Account Resources.** The Household Sales Account Resources field records the assigned sales team member resource for that particular household. Different contacts within a household can have different Sales Account Resources therefore this record is also relevant at the Contact level. A sales account team member has a defined access role.

Using Magic xpi Integration Platform, you can automate the creation (POST), deletion (DELETE), listing (GET), retrieval (GET), and updating (PATCH) of a Household Sales Account Resource. Information such as the access level, assignment type and function of the Household Sales Account Resource can be controlled here as well as the resource identifying attributes.

# 5 INTEGRATION WITH ORACLE SALES CLOUD ACCOUNTS

As with many **CRM** systems, **Oracle Sales Cloud** provides a comprehensive set of records to be managed in the lifetime of a customer relationship. Manually managing all of this data through a user interface screen can result in duplicate data entry, time consuming processes that detract from actual selling time, and inaccuracies due to human error. Whenever possible, enterprises should automate the integration between Oracle Sales Cloud and related enterprise and third party systems in order to optimize efficiency in accordance with best practice.

| Oracle Sales Cloud REST API: Account Resources |
| --- |
| Accounts |
|   Account Attachments |
|   Account Resources |
| Addresses |
|   Address Purposes |
| Aux Classifications |
| Notes |
| Primary Addresses |
| Relationships |
| Table 5:Account Resources |

**Magic xpi Integration Platform** users will be able to accomplish the required business process automation by dealing with all of the core objects and process of Oracle Sales Cloud related to Accounts, Contacts, Leads, Opportunities, Products, Activities, Partners, and so on.

Using the Magic xpi Studio, you can drag, drop and configure business processes that automate the handling of the **Oracle Sales Cloud Rest API**. Your business analysts will be able to build visual business process flows, specify data mapping and transformation, and control business logic according to your business rules. The integration can take place in scheduled batches or in real-time and near real-time events or services.

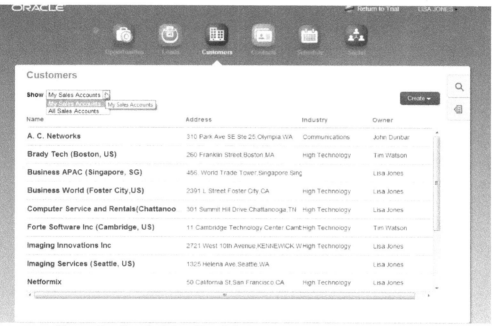

**Figure 5a.** Oracle Sales Cloud Accounts.

**Integrating Oracle Sales Cloud Accounts.** In Oracle Sales Cloud, an Account refers to an organization that your organizations sells to and can be either a prospect or a customer. Magic xpi can automate the creation (POST), deletion (DELETE), listing (GET), retrieval (GET), and updating (PATCH) of Accounts. Accounts are complex with many properties including nested children.

When getting an account, you can return just the link to the account or you can specify which account data to return. In Magic xpi Studio, be sure to pass the field parameter to filter the resource attributes. The Oracle Sales Cloud API will return only the specified attributes to Magic xpi. In a

29

situation where no attributes are specified, then no attributes will be returned. This could be used to get Account links only, for example. If an indirect child resource is passed as a field parameter, such as *Employees.Managers*, the unnamed children will be processed too.

You should be careful when deleting accounts. When you delete an account, the account status becomes inactive but the account record is not physically deleted from the database. It is withheld from account lists and searches. Child records such as attachments and notes to the account can no longer be viewed in Oracle Sales Cloud if the account is deleted. However, related objects such as opportunities, leads and tasks remain visible and you can still view the account name on these objects but not the account details.

**Account Resources.** Account resources are the team members of your organization assigned to an account. Magic xpi can automate the creation (POST), deletion (DELETE), listing (GET), retrieval (GET), and updating (PATCH) of Account Resources.

**Account Addresses.** Account addresses identify the physical location data of an account. Magic xpi can automate the creation (POST), deletion (DELETE), listing (GET), retrieval (GET), and updating (PATCH) of an Account Address.

**Account Notes.** An Account Note resource records information such as comments, descriptive information, or special instructions related to an account. A note is a record attached to a business object. Notes capture nonstandard information received as you do business, especially unstructured text. Magic xpi can automatically create (POST), delete (DELETE), get a list (GET), retrieve an individual note (GET), or update (PATCH) data that is pertaining to an Account Note.

**Account Primary Addresses.** The Account Primary Address capability built into Oracle Sales Cloud can be used by Magic xpi to view, create, and update the primary address for the location of an account. You can regard the primary address of an account as the default communication address of an account. Magic xpi can automate the creation (POST), deletion (DELETE), listing (GET), retrieval (GET), and updating (PATCH) of an Account Primary Addresses.

**Account Relationships.** Magic xpi can integrate with the Account Relationship resource to automatically manipulate account relationship information. An account relationship can have a status of active or inactive and Account Relationships can be of many different types such as Customer_Supplier or Customer_Subsidiary. Magic xpi can automate the creation (POST), listing (GET), and retrieval (GET) of an Account Relationship. The delete and update option are not available through the API for Account Relationships.

Once the desired flow logic has been created by your business analyst using the **Magic xpi Studio**, you can deploy your integration project to the **Magic xpi Integration Platform Server**. Activities on the server are managed in an **In-Memory Data Grid** that passes middleware messages in a redundant and highly scalable manner for maximum high availability and elastic scalability.

The deployed business process flows in your project can be monitored and the resulting metadata can be logged for performance monitoring and compliance purposes.

# 6 INTEGRATION WITH ORACLE SALES CLOUD CONTACTS

 **Oracle Sales Cloud** can be used to track relationships with customers, prospects and other individuals. In Oracle Sales Cloud, the primary data describing your customers and prospects are contained as *Accounts*, *Contacts*, and *Households*. These three types of records are interrelated and allow for the end-to-end recording and control of identifying information for your customers and prospects. People buy from people. So in many respects, your Contacts are your most important network. By understanding Oracle Sales Cloud Accounts, Contacts and Households, you can collect and present all of the relevant data for your contacts.

Oracle Sales Cloud deals with both customers and prospects. Customers and prospects can be organizations (accounts) and individuals (contacts), or a group of individuals (households). Magic xpi can perform **RESTful** and **SOAP Web Services** to integrate data and orchestrate processes related to Oracle Sales Cloud Contacts.

**Integrating Oracle Sales Cloud Contacts.** In Oracle Sales Cloud, a contact is a person. And contacts are in a defined relationship with either an account or another contact. Contacts can be involved in (B2C) or (B2B) sales. In Oracle Sales Cloud, a contact is not necessarily related to a current customer. For example, a salesperson may identify a prospect that they want to follow up with. In that case, the contact is a prospective customer or more simply put: a prospect.

There are numerous instances when contact data needs to be integrated and contact related business processes need to be orchestrated between different systems such as Oracle Cloud apps, other Oracle applications on-premise, and third-party cloud or on-premise applications. Since these relationships are usually not pre-defined, the business analyst is involved in identifying the gaps between the various data models, determining the system of record, the data relationships (master-slave, master-master, etc.) and determining the business process steps and workflow that needs to be automated in order to optimize the use of Oracle Sales Cloud.

| Oracle Sales Cloud REST API: Contact Resources |
| --- |
| Contacts |
|   Attachments |
|   Aux Classifications |
|   Contact Addresses |
|     Contact Address Purposes |
|   Contact Attachments |
|   Contact Primary Addresses |
|   Notes |
|   Relationships |
|   Sales Account Resources |
| Table 6:Contact Resources |

**Magic xpi Integration Platform** can use RESTful Web Services to automate the creation (POST), deletion (DELETE), listing (GET), retrieval (GET), and updating (PATCH) of Contacts in Oracle Sales Cloud. Magic xpi can leverage Oracle Sales Cloud SOAP Web Services to additionally merge, process and get the Entity list of Contacts in Oracle Sales Cloud.

**Contact Addresses.** In Oracle Sales Cloud, an address represents the location information of an account, contact, or household. In this case, we are discussing Contact Addresses. Magic xpi Integration Platform can be used to automate the creation (POST), deletion (DELETE), listing (GET), retrieval (GET), and updating (PATCH) of Contact Addresses in Oracle Sales Cloud.

**Contact Address Purpose.** In Oracle Sales Cloud, the purpose of an address is used to describe things such as SHIP_TO, BILL_TO, HOME_OFFICE, SHIPPING_YARD and other address purposes which are defined during setup. Magic xpi Integration Platform can be used to automate the creation (POST), deletion (DELETE), listing (GET), retrieval (GET), and updating (PATCH) of Contact Address Purposes in Oracle Sales Cloud.

**Contact Primary Addresses.** The Contact Primary Address capability built into Oracle Sales Cloud can be used by Magic xpi to view, create, and update the primary address for the location of a contact. You can regard the primary address of a contact as the default communication address of a contact. Magic xpi can automate the creation (POST), deletion (DELETE), listing (GET), retrieval (GET), and updating (PATCH) of a Contact Primary Addresses.

**Contact Notes.** The Contact Notes provide a means whereby a note can be associated to a Contact record in Oracle Sales Cloud. Using Magic xpi Integration Platform, you can automate the creation (POST), deletion (DELETE), listing (GET), retrieval (GET), and updating (PATCH) of a Contact Note. In addition to all of the relationship data and metadata, the core of a note is the NoteTxt field which is an unlimited string text field containing the actual Note text.

**Figure 6a.** Oracle Sales Cloud Contacts shown in user interface.

**Contact Relationships.** Contact Relationship Types are typically defined using the Setup and Maintenance area of the Oracle Sales Cloud application by an administrative user. Once defined, the Contact Relationships can be listed, viewed and created for any particular contact programmatically. In Oracle Sales Cloud, the Contact Relationship resource includes properties that are used to store values while viewing, creating, or updating a relationship. Using Magic xpi Integration Platform, you can automate the creation (POST), listing (GET), and retrieval (GET) of a Contact Relationship.

**Contacts Sales Account Resources.** The Contact Sales Account Resources field records the assigned sales team member resource for that particular contact. Different contacts within an account can have different Sales Account Resources therefore this record is also relevant at the Contact level. A sales account team member has a defined access role.

Using Magic xpi Integration Platform, you can automate the creation (POST), deletion (DELETE), listing (GET), retrieval (GET), and updating (PATCH) of a Contact Sales Account Resource. Information such as the access level, assignment type and function of the Contact Sales Account Resource can be controlled here as well as the resource identifying attributes.

As Contacts are one of the key objects in Oracle Sales Cloud, Magic xpi can be very useful in automating and orchestrating this and other objects used in any Oracle Sales Cloud implementation.

---

Hot Use Case:

Opportunity to Order Conversion

**Christie Digital Corporation**

A visual, audio and collaboration solutions company Christie employs over 1,500 people globally and has installed over 100,000 projection solutions for a variety of industries worldwide. As a leading manufacturer with global sales and distribution systems, Christie understands the value of synchronizing data and automating business processes across their IT systems.

Christie wanted a tool that would allow them to easily optimize business processes across Oracle Sales Cloud and their other business applications, including Oracle JD Edwards ERP, Oracle Agile PLM, Microsoft SharePoint and their corporate website.

Closed sales orders on opportunities in Oracle Sales Cloud need to be automatically converted to orders in JD Edwards ERP. This is opportunity to order conversion and is a very common requirement. Magic xpi makes automation of such processes much easier.

"Magic's graphic work flow approach makes development .more straightforward. Programmers are able to do complicated things easily, with a single skill set. Development time is reduced. Business benefits are experienced sooner, and the resulting system can be adapted quicker using fewer resources."

■ Darrell Kieswetter, former Technical Operations Manager

---

# 7 INTEGRATION WITH ORACLE SALES CLOUD OPPORTUNITIES

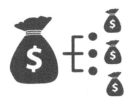 Every **CRM** system and sales organization deals with *Opportunities*. In **Oracle Sales Cloud**, the opportunities resource in the **Oracle Sales Cloud REST API** lets your developers or business analysts view, create, and update an opportunity. In Oracle Sales Cloud, an opportunity supports the end-to-end sales continuum spanning leads, opportunities, orders, and follow-up activities. Within any given opportunity record, your sales organizations can store information about a wide variety of characteristics related to an opportunity, such as the account, sales team and products to be sold.

| Oracle Sales Cloud REST API: Opportunity Resources |
|---|
| Opportunities |
|   Notes |
|   Opportunity Competitors |
|   Opportunity Contacts |
|   Opportunity Deals |
|   Opportunity Leads |
|   Opportunity Partners |
|   Opportunity Sources |
|   Opportunity Team Members |
|   Revenue Items |
|     Opportunity Revenue Territories |
|     Product Groups |
|     Products |
| Table 7:Opportunity Resources |

**Opportunities.** In Oracle Sales Cloud, an Opportunity contains the information about a specific potential sale to an account and contains information regarding the lead, follow-up activities, account information, products-to-be-sold and so on. Magic xpi can automate the creation (POST), deletion (DELETE), listing (GET), retrieval (GET), and updating (PATCH) of an Opportunity.

**Opportunity Notes.** In Oracle Sales Cloud, an Opportunity Note resource records information such as comments, descriptive information, or special instructions related to an opportunity. A note is a record attached to a business object. Notes capture nonstandard information received as you do business, especially unstructured text. Magic xpi can automatically create (POST), delete (DELETE), get a list (GET), retrieve an individual note (GET), or update (PATCH) data that is pertaining to an Opportunity Note.

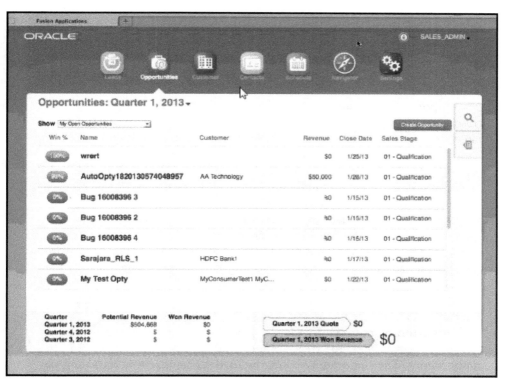

**Figure 7a.** Oracle Sales Cloud User Interface: Opportunities.

**Opportunity Competitors.** In Oracle Sales Cloud, an opportunity competitor resource allows you to view, create, and update any of the competitors for an opportunity. With the opportunity competitors resource,

Oracle Sales Cloud can store information about the competitors associated with the opportunity. Magic xpi can automatically create (POST), delete (DELETE), get a list (GET), retrieve an individual competitor (GET), or update (PATCH) data that is pertaining to an Opportunity Competitor.

**Opportunity Contacts.** In Oracle Sales Cloud, an opportunity contact resource allows you to view, create, and update any of the contacts within the account relevant to an opportunity. With the opportunity contact resource, Oracle Sales Cloud can store information about the contacts associated directly to a specific opportunity. Magic xpi can automatically create (POST), delete (DELETE), get a list (GET), retrieve an individual competitor (GET), or update (PATCH) data that is pertaining to an Opportunity Contact.

**Opportunity Deals.** In Oracle Sales Cloud, a deal registration creates a registered partner deal that is associated to an opportunity. Deal registration is a process by which a partner user registers a business opportunity with the brand owner in order to become eligible for benefits, such as exclusive rights to the opportunity, additional rebates, presales support, and so on. With the opportunity deals resource, Oracle Sales Cloud can retrieve information about the registered deals. Magic xpi can automatically get a list (GET) or retrieve an individual deal (GET) that is pertaining to an Opportunity.

**Opportunity Leads.** In Oracle Sales Cloud, an opportunity lead resource allows you to view, create, and update any of the leads relevant to an opportunity. With the opportunity lead resource, Oracle Sales Cloud can store information about the leads associated directly to a specific opportunity. Magic xpi can automatically create (POST), delete (DELETE), get a list (GET), retrieve an individual lead (GET), or update (PATCH) data that is pertaining to an Opportunity Lead.

**Opportunity Partner.** In Oracle Sales Cloud, an opportunity revenue partner resource allows you to view, create, and update any of the partners associated with this opportunity. The opportunity partner is used to store information about partners who are contributing to the selling effort of the current opportunity. Magic xpi can automatically create (POST), delete (DELETE), get a list (GET), retrieve an individual partner (GET), or update (PATCH) data that is pertaining to an Opportunity Partner.

**Opportunity Source.** In Oracle Sales Cloud, an opportunity source resource allows you to view, create, and update the source of an opportunity. The opportunity source is used to capture the marketing or sales campaign that resulted in this opportunity. Magic xpi can automatically create (POST), delete (DELETE), get a list of sources (GET), retrieve an individual source (GET), or update (PATCH) source data that is pertaining to an Opportunity.

**Opportunity Team Members.** In Oracle Sales Cloud, an opportunity team member resource allows you to view, create, and update the sales team members participating in an opportunity. Magic xpi can automatically create (POST), delete (DELETE), get a list of team members (GET), retrieve an individual team member (GET), or update (PATCH) team member data that is pertaining to an Opportunity.

**Opportunity Revenue Items.** In Oracle Sales Cloud, an opportunity revenue item resource allows you to view, create, and update revenue items of an opportunity. The revenue items associated with opportunities are products, services, or other items a customer might be interested in purchasing. You add revenue items by selecting a product group or product to associate with an opportunity. Magic xpi can automatically create (POST), delete (DELETE), get a list of revenue items (GET), retrieve an individual revenue item (GET), or update (PATCH) revenue item data that is pertaining to an Opportunity.

**Opportunity Revenue Territories.** In Oracle Sales Cloud, an opportunity revenue territory exists as a child record to an opportunity revenue item. The revenue territory resource allows you to view, create, and update revenue territories of items in an opportunity. Magic xpi can automatically create (POST), delete (DELETE), get a list of revenue territories (GET), retrieve an individual revenue territory (GET), or update (PATCH) revenue territory data that is pertaining to an Opportunity.

**Opportunity Products.** In Oracle Sales Cloud, the Products business object defines the goods and service you sell. Using Magic xpi, your business analyst may automate the creation listing (GET) of product groups and retrieval (GET) of a specific product group associated to an opportunity. Using Magic xpi, your business analyst or developer can also automatically capture the name of the product group associated with the opportunity.

**Opportunity Product Groups.** In Oracle Sales Cloud, the Product Groups business objects are used to associate similar products. Using Magic xpi, your business analyst may automate the creation listing (GET) of product groups and retrieval (GET) of a specific product group associated to an opportunity. Using Magic xpi, your business analyst or developer can also automatically capture the name of the product group associated with the opportunity.

The ability automate business processes based on opportunity information is important not only for synchronization between systems but also for maintaining key event driven triggers for business process automation such as an opportunity to order conversion between Oracle Sales Cloud opportunities and your ERP system.

# 8 INTEGRATION WITH ORACLE SALES CLOUD FORECASTS AND SALES ORDERS

**Oracle Sales Cloud** offers sophisticated forecasting capabilities so that an organization can provide predictions of future revenue for a specific period of time. This information is valuable to an organization for general planning, production scheduling, and for providing guidance to owners and investors. Forecasts are built from data by territory and are specific to a period of time such as a month, quarter or year. Similar to other CRM systems, a forecast is information related to the likelihood of an order and an order contains the detailed lines, prices (revenue items or items) and terms in the order itself. In Oracle Sales Cloud, a Sales Order is really a quotation or quote. Once the opportunity closes, the quote becomes an order. This will trigger the need for integration with accounting and ERP systems as well as fulfillment, logistics and other systems in the organization.

The **Oracle Sales Cloud REST API** allows you to automate and integrate processes related to *Forecasts* and *Sales Orders*. The API allows you to view and edit forecast items programmatically but it does not allow for the creation of deletion of forecast data through the API. This limitation

---

**Hot Use Case: Quote Integration**

**Pacific Steel & Recycling**

Pacific Steel & Recycling uses Magic xpi to integrate to Quote, QuoteItem and QuoteAddress. "Magic xpi Integration Platform is known for its excellent [Oracle] Adapter but what impressed me was its ability to automate discovery and handling of APIs that are completely unknown to it. This is a great tool for API integration to 3rd party software."

*-Kenneth Hess, CIO, Pacific Steel and Recycling*

---

is there to preserve the integrity of the forecast and force forecast data to be based on user input as well as to prohibit deletion of initial forecast data (it can however be modified).

| Oracle Sales Cloud REST API: Forecast and Sales Orders Resources |
| --- |
| Forecast |
|    Adjustment Periods |
|    Forecast Items |
|    Forecast Products |
|       Product Adjustment Periods |
| Sales Orders (Quotes) |
| Table 8:Forecast and Sales Orders Resources |

**Forecasts.** In Oracle Sales Cloud, the API resource for Forecasts allows you to work with individual forecasts or a list of all forecasts. You use the API to get a list of forecasts so that you can then programmatically examine each item in the list recursively. A forecast has adjustment periods, items, item details, products, and so on. Magic xpi can automate the listing (GET), retrieval (GET), and updating (PATCH) of a Forecast.

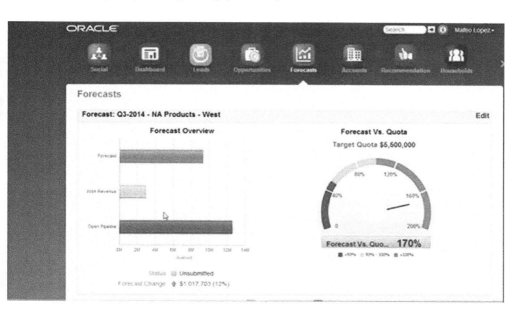

**Figure 8a.** Oracle Sales Cloud user interface: Forecast Dashboard.

**Adjustment Periods.** In Oracle Sales Cloud, an adjustment period is the specific span of time for which you need to modify or adjust a sales forecast. An opportunity which had been rated at 20% chance of close may need to be adjusted upward to 50% chance of closing, for example. The adjustment periods resource allows you to work with these changes to the forecast in an automated fashion. Magic xpi can automate the listing (GET), retrieval (GET), and updating (PATCH) of an Adjustment Periods. This will include information about the *PeriodId*, the *ParticipantId*, the items to be adjusted, and so on.

**Forecast Items.** In Oracle Sales Cloud, Forecast Items contain the specific revenue item details of the opportunity that you wish to include in the forecast. Magic xpi can automate the listing (GET), retrieval (GET), and updating (PATCH) of a Forecast Items.

**Forecast Products.** In Oracle Sales Cloud, the Forecast Products is the product associated to a revenue item. The API resource displays the forecast by product. Magic xpi can automate the listing (GET), retrieval (GET), and updating (PATCH) of a Forecast Products. Forecast Products may have nested Product Adjustment Periods.

**Product Adjustment Periods.** In Oracle Sales Cloud, the Product Adjustment Period is the span of time for the changed Forecast Product. The API resource provides visibility to a forecast product and the ability to update it.

**Sales Orders.** In Oracle Sales Cloud, the API resource for Sales Orders allows you to work with sales quotes. Magic xpi can automate the creation (POST), deletion (DELETE), listing (GET), retrieval (GET), and updating (PATCH) of Sales Orders.

# 9 INTEGRATION WITH ORACLE SALES CLOUD ACTIVITIES

One of the primary purposes of **CRM** systems is to keep track of sales activities with prospects and customers. In **Oracle Sales Cloud**, an *Activity* record stores all of the information related to appointments, meetings and tasks. Like the tickler systems of the past, CRM systems remind us when to be in contact with our prospects and customers, but with a much greater degree of sophistication than mere interval reminders.

| Oracle Sales Cloud REST API: Activities Resources |
|---|
| Activities |
|   Activity Assignees |
|   Activity Attachments |
|   Activity Contacts |
|   Activity Objectives |
|   Notes |
| Table 9:Activities Resources |

With Oracle Sales Cloud features for Activity Management the system can guide your sales team members to pursue objectives and accomplish key tasks and important milestones along the way to obtaining an order and making a sale related to a particular opportunity. With user level features built into the Oracle Sales Cloud interface a fairly straightforward sales methodology is available without resorting to spreadsheets or other apps to monitor and record selling activities such as appointments, meetings and tasks. **Oracle CX Cloud** includes Oracle Sales Cloud and offers the functionality to allow all of your sales team to become increasingly proficient in managing sales activities and following sales methodology along a defined sales arc. As sales managers find that they have more insight with Oracle Sales Cloud they can balance talents, be more productive in pursuing sales and revenue objectives and find the competitive edge needed.

**Magic xpi Integration Platform** gives you the ability to automate and integrate the task and appointment information contained in Oracle Sales Cloud Activities. Business Analysts in your IT organization can set up established rules contained in business process flows that determine when, how and what Activity data to pull, record, automate and share. In today's blog article, let's look at how-to integrate and manage business processes around Oracle Sales Cloud Activities.

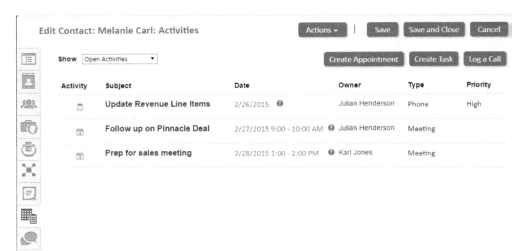

**Figure 9a.** Oracle Sales Cloud user interface: Activities.

**Integrating Oracle Sales Cloud Activities.** Magic xpi can work with all of your Oracle Sales Cloud activities. In Oracle Sales Cloud, Activities capture the task and appointment information. Magic xpi can automate the creation (POST), deletion (DELETE), listing (GET), retrieval (GET), and updating (PATCH) of Activities. Activities contain items as a root schema as well as a number of nested schemas: Activity Assignee; Activity Contacts; Activity Objectives; Activity Assignee Items, Activity Contact Items; Activity Objective Items; Activity Note Items and the various links associated with them. This provides a wealth of integration touch points available to the Magic xpi Business Analyst and developer. Keep in mind that each activity has a unique identifying number and that this number may be externally generated.

When retrieving activities, the finder parameter is a very useful tool for refining which activities are retrieved. Magic xpi can find:
- *call reports* related to a past appointment
- *appointments* within a data range
- *activities* where a specified user is a resource
- activities in a *completed status*
- a *list* of call reports
- *tasks owned* by a specified user
- *call reports* within a date range
- *appointments not having* an associated call report
- all *open* activities
- activities where a specified *contact is defined*
- activities with a *specified activity number*, and
- an activity with a *specified primary key* identifier.

**Activity Assignees.** The activity assignees are the resources associated to an activity in Oracle Sales Cloud. Magic xpi can automate the creation (POST), deletion (DELETE), listing (GET), retrieval (GET), and updating (PATCH) of Activity Assignees.

**Activity Contacts.** The activity contacts are the customer or prospect Contacts associated to an activity in Oracle Sales Cloud. Magic xpi can automate the creation (POST), deletion (DELETE), listing (GET), retrieval (GET), and updating (PATCH) of Activity Contacts.

**Activity Objectives.** The activity Objectives are the sales objectives associated to an activity in Oracle Sales Cloud. Magic xpi can automate the creation (POST), deletion (DELETE), listing (GET), retrieval (GET), and updating (PATCH) of Activity Objectives. Objectives can have a status of Complete or Incomplete. Completed activities have a Boolean value of TRUE. Activity Objectives are categorized by an Objective Code and described by freeform text.

**Activity Notes.** The activity notes are the note data object that captures comments, information or instructions related to an activity in Oracle Sales Cloud. Magic xpi can automate the creation (POST), deletion (DELETE), listing (GET), retrieval (GET), and updating (PATCH) of Activity Notes.

By combining these capabilities, Magic xpi provides full automation and management capabilities to Business Analysts using the Magic xpi Studio to define effective business process integration for Oracle Sales Cloud in the Oracle CX Cloud.

Integrating activity information to third party marketing automation platforms such as *Marketo, Hubspot, Silverpop, InfusionSoft, Unica, Teradata/aprimo, pardot, SimplyCast, acton, SIGNAL, genius, Manticore* and others can be accomplished using Magic xpi Integration Platform.

# 10 INTEGRATION WITH ORACLE SALES CLOUD PRODUCTS

 Within the **Oracle CX Cloud**, the **Oracle Sales Cloud** includes product definition and product management features available at the administrator, end-user and API level through a products interface. Your business or organization may import products from external systems using a file-based data import tool or you can use Web services to create products directly in Oracle Sales Cloud by synchronizing with other systems where the product data originates. Oracle Sales Cloud *Products* can be integrated with Enterprise Resource Planning (**ERP**) systems, Product Lifecycle Management (**PLM**) systems and other enterprise systems where product information is tracked.

| Oracle Sales Cloud REST API: Products Resources |
| --- |
| Products |
| Price Book Headers |
| Price Book Items |
| Product Groups |
| Attachments |
| Filter Attributes |
| Filter Attribute Values |
| Products |
| Related Groups |
| Subgroups |
| Table 10:Products Resources |

Utilizing the **Magic xpi Integration Platform** these capabilities can be automated in a code-free, drag and drop interface that allows business analysts and developers in your IT department to set up end-to-end product lifecycle and sales lifecycle integration.

Let's look at the specifics of how Magic xpi Integration Platform can automate Oracle Sales Cloud *Products* integration:

**Products.** In Oracle Sales Cloud, the product resource is used to view, create, or modify a product. A product is something that your company wants to sell. In Oracle Sales Cloud, once you create a product, you cannot delete it. However, you can "hide" products in consuming applications by adjusting the Eligible to Sell property. Using Magic xpi, your business analyst or developer may automate the creation (POST), listing (GET), retrieval (GET), and updating (PATCH) of Products.

**Prices.** In Oracle Sales Cloud, you can manage prices directly from within Oracle Sales Cloud or by using the more complex and powerful **Oracle CPQ Cloud** (Configure, Price, Quote). We describe here the internal **Oracle Sales Cloud REST API** functionality for pricing as it relates to products. Price Books have headers and items. The header contains information about the price book generally and the items contain information about the prices of individual prices.

**Price Book Headers.** The Price Book Header resource is used to view, create, update, and delete the name, description, and status of a price book. It also includes the unique identifier, unique code, and the currency on which the price book amount is based. Using Magic xpi, your business analyst may automate the creation (POST), deletion (DELETE), listing (GET), retrieval (GET), and updating (PATCH) of Price Book Headers.

**Price Book Items.** In Oracle Sales Cloud, Price Book Items act as a resource associating products with prices. Using Magic xpi, your business analyst may automate the creation (POST), deletion (DELETE), listing (GET), retrieval (GET), and updating (PATCH) of Price Book Headers.

**Product Groups.** In Oracle Sales Cloud, a Product Group is a business object that contains related products. An example of a product group name is Men's Fashion that includes all of your clothing and accessories products for men so that customers can browse through all the products in this group in your product catalog. Using Magic xpi, your business analyst may automate the creation (POST), deletion (DELETE), listing (GET), retrieval (GET), and updating (PATCH) of Product Groups.

In Oracle Sales Cloud, locking a product group makes it inaccessible or non editable by others while you are making changes. Magic xpi can use the creation (POST) function to lock a product group, publish a list of all locked product groups, or release the lock on a product group. Publishing the product group makes the changes available to the users at runtime.

**Product Group Attachments.** In Oracle Sales Cloud, a Product Group may contain attachments. Using Magic xpi, your business analyst may automate the creation (POST), deletion (DELETE), listing (GET), retrieval (GET), and updating (PATCH) of Product Group Attachments.

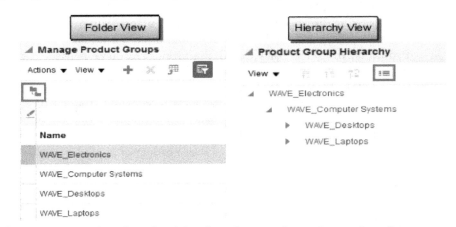

**Figure 10a.** Oracle Sales Cloud Product Groups shown in user interface.

**Product Group Filter Attributes.** In Oracle Sales Cloud, the Filter Attributes resource is used to aid in the designation of product characteristics within a Product Group. Examples of Product Group Filter Attributes are size, color, and fabric. Using Magic xpi, your business analyst may automate the creation (POST), deletion (DELETE), retrieval (GET), and updating (PATCH) of Product Group Filter Attributes.

**Product Group Products.** In Oracle Sales Cloud, a Product Group Products resource associates an actual product to the lowest level product group to which it belongs. Using Magic xpi, your business analyst may automate the creation (POST), deletion (DELETE), listing (GET), retrieval (GET), and updating (PATCH) of Product Group Products.

**Product Groups Subgroups.** A product group can exist in relationship to other product groups as a parent or child product group association. A sub product group can belong to a product group. Women's Pants can be a Sub Product Group of Women's Fashion which in turn can be a sub product group of Fashion. Products Groups Subgroups is used to create a subgroup and its association. Using Magic xpi, your business analyst or developer may automate the creation (POST), deletion (DELETE), listing (GET), retrieval (GET), and updating (PATCH) of Product Groups Subgroups.

**Product Groups Related Groups.** In Oracle Sales Cloud, Products Groups Related Groups is used to define the nature of that association, not to create the actual subgroup, but rather to designate its association. Using Magic xpi, your business analyst or developer may automate the creation

(POST), deletion (DELETE), listing (GET), retrieval (GET), and updating (PATCH) of Product Groups Related Groups associations.

Using the various Products, Prices, and Product Groups capabilities of Oracle Sales Cloud, Magic xpi can provide a high degree of business process automation for organizations deploying Oracle CX Cloud/Oracle Sales Cloud. These interface and integration capabilities give developers and business analysts the tools they need to transform business processes and keep Oracle Sales Cloud synchronized with ERP, PLM, CPQ and other systems.

# 11 INTEGRATION WITH ORACLE SALES CLOUD PARTNERS

When comparing the capabilities of **Oracle CX Cloud** and **Oracle Sales Cloud** in particular to that of other **CRM** systems it compares well in terms of partner relationship management data tracking. Using **Magic xpi Integration Platform** a business analyst or programmer analyst in your information technology department should be able to integrate data and orchestrate processes dealing with Oracle Sales Cloud *Partners*.

| Oracle Sales Cloud REST API: Partners Resources |
|---|
| Partners |
|   Attachments |
|   Expertises |
|   Focus Areas |
|   Geographies |
|   Industries |
|   Notes |
|   Product Account Team Members |
|   Partner Certifications |
|   Partner Contacts |
|     User Account Details |
|   Partner Types |
| Table 11:Partners Resources |

**Partners.** In Oracle Sales Cloud, partners are companies that work with your organization to help sell your products and services. Magic xpi can automate the creation (POST), listing (GET), retrieval (GET), and updating (PATCH) of Partners.

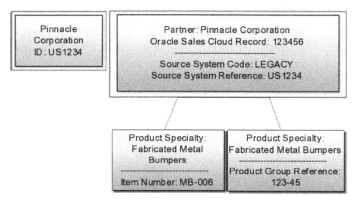

**Figure 11a. Sample Partner ID and reference data relationships for file imports.**

Each partner record contains an extensive number of fields that contain information about your sales partner as well as any number of child records for the account. The integration complexity is deep yet powerful in all that it allows your organization to track about your partners. Oracle Sales Cloud is actually used by Oracle to manage partner relationships among its massive partner community known as the Oracle Partner Network or OPN. Descriptions of the integration possible with the child records of the Oracle Sales Cloud Partner record follows:

**Partner Attachments.** In Oracle Sales Cloud, a partner record may contain attachments. Using Magic xpi, your business analyst may automate the creation (POST), deletion (DELETE), listing (GET), retrieval (GET), and updating (PATCH) of Partner Attachments.

**Partner Expertises.** In Oracle Sales Cloud, a partner record may contain information about the expertise of your sales partner. This is usually self-declared by the partner. Using Magic xpi, you can automate the creation (POST), deletion (DELETE), listing (GET), retrieval (GET), and updating (PATCH) of Partner Expertises.

**Partner Focus Areas.** In Oracle Sales Cloud, a partner record may contain information about the market or sales focus areas of your partners. This is normally self-selected by the partner. Using Magic xpi, you can create automated flows that manage the creation (POST), deletion (DELETE), listing (GET), retrieval (GET), and updating (PATCH) of Partner Focus Areas.

**Partner Geographies.** In Oracle Sales Cloud, A partner geography resource is used to view, create, or modify the geographies that the partner operates in, such as, United States or Florida. A partner record may contain information about the geographic areas of your partners. Using Magic xpi, you can create automated flows that manage the creation (POST), deletion (DELETE), listing (GET), retrieval (GET), and updating (PATCH) of Partner Geographies.

**Partner Industries.** In Oracle Sales Cloud, a partner record may contain information about the industries targeted or served by your partners such as manufacturing or healthcare. Using Magic xpi, you can create automated flows that manage the creation (POST), deletion (DELETE), listing (GET), retrieval (GET), and updating (PATCH) of Partner Industries.

**Partner Notes.** In Oracle Sales Cloud, a partner record may contain notes related to your sales partner. Using Magic xpi, you can automate the creation (POST), deletion (DELETE), listing (GET), retrieval (GET), and updating (PATCH) of Partner Notes. Partner Notes are based on cURL.

**Partner Account Team Members.** In Oracle Sales Cloud, a partner record contains a child record with information about the persons in your organization who manage a partner account and can edit the partner information. Using Magic xpi, you can create automated flows that manage the creation (POST), deletion (DELETE), listing (GET), retrieval (GET), and updating (PATCH) of Partner Account Team Members.

**Partner Certifications.** In Oracle Sales Cloud, a partner record may contain information about the certifications earned by your sales partner. This is usually earned by the partner or awarded by your company after some combination of training and examination. Using Magic xpi, you can automate the creation (POST), deletion (DELETE), listing (GET), retrieval (GET), and updating (PATCH) of Partner Certifications.

**Partner Contacts.** In Oracle Sales Cloud, a partner record contains child records with information about persons in the partner organization. Using Magic xpi, you can create automated flows that manage the creation (POST), deletion (DELETE), listing (GET), retrieval (GET), and updating (PATCH) of Partner Contacts. In addition, Magic xpi can automate the creation (POST), deletion (DELETE), listing (GET), retrieval (GET), and updating (PATCH) of Partner Contact User Account Details.

**Partner Type.** In Oracle Sales Cloud, a partner record may contain information about the partner type such as dealer, OEM or franchisee. Using Magic xpi, you can automate the creation (POST), deletion (DELETE), listing (GET), and retrieval (GET) of Partner Types. Partner Type may not be changed using an Update (PATCH) function.

In addition to the integration and business process flow capabilities made possible by these API capabilities of Magic xpi for Oracle Sales Cloud Partners, Magic xpi can work with the features for Oracle Sales Cloud *Partner Tiers* and Oracle Sales Cloud *Partner Programs*.

# 12 INTEGRATION WITH ORACLE SALES CLOUD PARTNER PROGRAMS

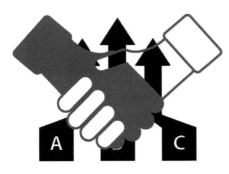

In **Oracle Sales Cloud**, we have discussed the excellent Partner Relationship Management capabilities of the system. In fact, there are really three methods by which a prospective partner can become a partner. Prospective partners or companies that have an interest in a partnership relationship with your company can either use the *Self Service Partner Registration* business process flow to submit a customizable application to become a registered partner; or your sales channel team members can manually create a partner from a new or existing customer record; or Magic xpi Integration Platform can automatically use the capabilities of the **Oracle Sales Cloud REST API** to do the same.

For more on that discussion, see the previous chapter. In this chapter on Oracle Sales Cloud features for Partner Programs, we will focus on Program Benefits and Program Enrollments. In Oracle Sales Cloud, if the channel organization offers partner programs, a partner can enroll into a partner program and receive the benefits associated with the program. A partner program enrollment goes through many statuses during its lifecycle.

**Enrollments.** An enrollment can be automated and may be entered in a self service web page or by Oracle Sales Cloud users. It can exist in any of these statuses:

• Approved. In Oracle Sales Cloud, an approved enrollment is active and is within the date of expiration for the program.

• Expired. In Oracle Sales Cloud, an expired partner program enrollment has an enrollment end date and has gone beyond the end date of the program.

• Renewed. In Oracle Sales Cloud, this is when the partner has renewed the enrollment.

• Rejected. In Oracle Sales Cloud, this is an enrollment request that was rejected. Approvers can reject or approve an enrollment at their discretion based on the contract, responses to questionnaire, and so on.

• Terminated. In Oracle Sales Cloud, this is a partner program enrollment that was terminated. Termination can occur at the supplier's discretion or when a program is decommissioned.

• Pending Approval. The partner has submitted a request for enrollment, but the enrollment has not yet been approved.

| Oracle Sales Cloud REST API: Partner Programs Resources |
| --- |
| Partner Programs |
|   Countries |
| Program Benefits |
|   Benefit List Details |
| …Program Benefit Details |
|   Program Enrollments |
|   Program Enrollment Notes |

Table 12:Partner Programs Resources

**Partner Programs.** In Oracle Sales Cloud, the partner program resource is used to view, create, and update information about partner programs such as the name of the program, program description, validity period, and so on. With Magic xpi Integration Platform, you can automatically retrieve (GET) and list (GET) the partner program(s) for the enrollment. This allows you to see: the user who created the program record; the date and time when the program record was created; indicates if the record can be deleted; see the effective date when the program ends; the date and time when the program record was last updated; the user who updated the program record; the unique Identifier of the partner program associated with the enrollment (this is the primary key of the partner program table); the description of the program; the unique identifier of the person managing the partner program; the name of the program manager; the name of the partner program; the unique number generated for the program; indicates the type of the partner program (the accepted values are reseller and go to market); the effective date when the program starts; and indicates if the record can be updated.

**Program Benefits.** In Oracle Sales Cloud, Program Benefits is the Web service used to manage program benefits in the Benefits Library for addition to partner programs. Using Magic xpi, your business analyst or developer may automate the creation (POST), deletion (DELETE), listing (GET), retrieval (GET), and updating (PATCH) of Partner Program Program Benefits.

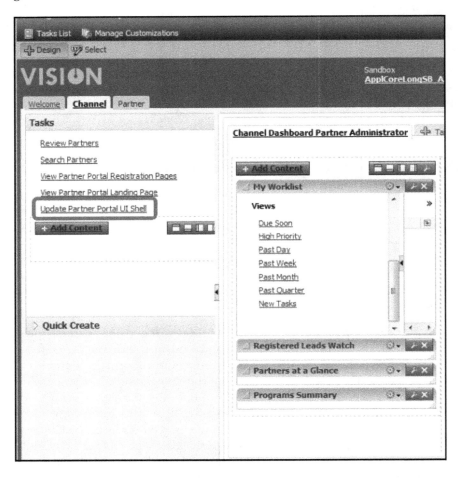

**Figure 12a.** Partner Program materials as they may appear in user interface.

**Benefit List Values.** In Oracle Sales Cloud, Benefit List Values is the Web service child of program benefits that is used to manage benefit list values to list the type of benefits in the partner program. Using Magic xpi, your business analyst or developer may automate the creation (POST), deletion (DELETE), listing (GET), retrieval (GET), and updating (PATCH) of Partner Program Benefit List Values.

**Program Enrollments.** In Oracle Sales Cloud, Program Enrollments is the Web service used to view, create, or update partner enrollments in a particular partner program. Once enrolled, a partner is not deleted from a program enrollment. However, program enrollment status may change. The accepted status values are draft, pending, approved, rejected, terminated, and renewed. Using Magic xpi, your business analyst or developer may automate the creation (POST), listing (GET), retrieval (GET), and updating (PATCH) of Partner Program Program Enrollments.

**Program Enrollment Notes.** In Oracle Sales Cloud, the note resource is used to capture comments, information, or instructions for a program enrollment. Using Magic xpi, your business analyst may automate the creation (POST), deletion (DELETE), listing (GET), retrieval (GET), and updating (PATCH) of Program Enrollment Notes.

# 13 INTEGRATION WITH ORACLE SALES CLOUD PARTNER PROGRAM ENROLLMENTS AND BENEFITS

In **Oracle Sales Cloud**, we have discussed the excellent Partner Relationship Management capabilities of the system. In fact, there are really three methods by which a prospective partner can become a partner. Prospective partners or companies that have an interest in a partnership relationship with your company can either use the *Self Service Partner Registration* business process flow to submit a customizable application to become a registered partner; or your sales channel team members can manually create a partner from a new or existing customer record; or Magic xpi Integration Platform can automatically use the capabilities of the **Oracle Sales Cloud REST API** to do the same.

| Oracle Sales Cloud REST API: Partner Program Enrollments and Benefits Resources |
| --- |
| Partner Programs |
| Program Benefits |
| Benefit List Values |
| Program Enrollments |

Table 13:Partner Program Enrollments and Resources

For more on that discussion, see the previous chapter. In this chapter on Oracle Sales Cloud features for Partner Programs, we will focus on Program Benefits and Program Enrollments. In Oracle Sales Cloud, if the channel organization offers partner programs, a partner can enroll into a partner program and receive the benefits associated with the program. A partner program enrollment goes through many statuses during its lifecycle.

An enrollment can be automated and may be entered in a self service web page or by Oracle Sales Cloud users. It can exist in any of these statuses:

• *Approved.* In Oracle Sales Cloud, an approved enrollment is active and is within the date of expiration for the program.

• *Expired.* In Oracle Sales Cloud, an expired partner program enrollment has an enrollment end date and has gone beyond the end date of the program.

• *Renewed.* In Oracle Sales Cloud, this is when the partner has renewed the enrollment.

• *Rejected.* In Oracle Sales Cloud, this is an enrollment request that was rejected. Approvers can reject or approve an enrollment at their discretion based on the contract, responses to questionnaire, and so on.

• *Terminated.* In Oracle Sales Cloud, this is a partner program enrollment that was terminated. Termination can occur at the supplier's discretion or when a program is decommissioned.

• *Pending Approval.* The partner has submitted a request for enrollment, but the enrollment has not yet been approved.

**Partner Programs.** In Oracle Sales Cloud, the partner program resource is used to view, create, and update information about partner programs such as the name of the program, program description, validity period, and so on. With Magic xpi Integration Platform, you can automatically retrieve (GET) and list (GET) the partner program(s) for the enrollment. This allows you to see: the user who created the program record; the date and time when the program record was created; indicates if the record can be deleted; see the effective date when the program ends; the date and time when the program record was last updated; the user who updated the program record; the unique Identifier of the partner program associated with the enrollment (this is the primary key of the partner program table); the description of the program; the unique identifier of the person managing the partner program; the name of the program manager; the name of the partner program; the unique number generated for the program; indicates the type of the partner program (the accepted values are reseller and go to market); the effective date when the program starts; and indicates if the record can be updated.

**Program Benefits.** In Oracle Sales Cloud, Program Benefits is the Web service used to manage program benefits in the Benefits Library for addition to partner programs. Using Magic xpi, your business analyst or developer may automate the creation (POST), deletion (DELETE), listing (GET), retrieval (GET), and updating (PATCH) of Partner Program Program Benefits.

**Benefit List Values.** In Oracle Sales Cloud, Benefit List Values is the Web service child of program benefits that is used to manage benefit list values to list the type of benefits in the partner program. Using Magic xpi, your business analyst or developer may automate the creation (POST), deletion (DELETE), listing (GET), retrieval (GET), and updating (PATCH) of Partner Program Benefit List Values.

**Program Enrollments.** In Oracle Sales Cloud, Program Enrollments is the Web service used to view, create, or update partner enrollments in a particular partner program. Once enrolled, a partner is not deleted from a program enrollment. However, program enrollment status may change. The accepted status values are draft, pending, approved, rejected, terminated, and renewed. Using Magic xpi, your business analyst or developer may automate the creation (POST), listing (GET), retrieval (GET), and updating (PATCH) of Partner Program Program Enrollments.

Program Enrollment Notes. In Oracle Sales Cloud, the note resource is used to capture comments, information, or instructions for a program enrollment. Using Magic xpi, your business analyst may automate the creation (POST), deletion (DELETE), listing (GET), retrieval (GET), and updating (PATCH) of Program Enrollment Notes.

# 14 INTEGRATION WITH ORACLE SALES CLOUD DEAL REGISTRATIONS

One of the benefits of the strong partner relationship management features in **Oracle Sales Cloud** is its capabilities for **Deal Registration**. The Deal Registration feature in Oracle Sales Cloud allows a business partner of your company to use Oracle Sales Cloud to register a deal with your company. By registering the deal, the partner provides certain details about a lead and opportunity (deal) and gains certain benefits by doing so. These benefits are normally specified by your company in a written partner contract or agreement signed by the partner and your company.

| Oracle Sales Cloud REST API: Deal Registration Resources |
| --- |
| Deal Registrations |
| Deal Products |
| Deal Team Members |
| Notes |
| Opportunities |
| Product Groups |
| Products |
| Table 14:Deal Registrations |

Benefits of deal registration may include exclusive rights to an opportunity for a period of time, quota credit, earned discount levels, incentive and loyalty program points, sales support benefits, and customer benefits such as a superior level of service.

The Oracle Sales Cloud REST API delivers strong capabilities for managing the registration of deals in an automated fashion. Magic xpi Integration Platform leverages the API to automate deal registration processes.

**Deal Registration.** The deal registration resource avails a process by which a partner user registers a business opportunity with the brand owner in order to request benefits such as exclusivity in an opportunity, quota credit, presales support, and loyalty points. Using Magic xpi, your business analyst may automatically create (POST), list (GET), retrieve (GET), and update (PATCH) of Program Enrollment Notes. Registered deals may not be deleted using the API.

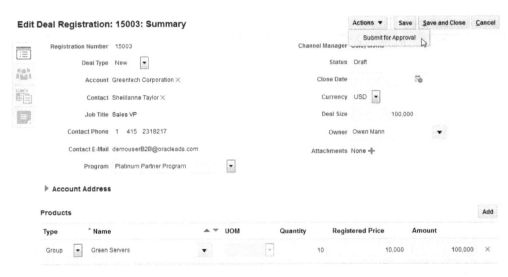

**Figure 14a.** Deal Registrations as shown in the user interface.

**Deal Products.** In order to register a deal, you would normally declare the products that are in the opportunity. Deal Products contains the information about the products in the registered deal. This resource can be automated by Magic xpi to help create deal products (POST), delete deal products (DELETE), list and retrieve deal products (GET) and update a previously created deal product (PATCH).

**Deal Team Members.** In Oracle Sales Cloud, a deal team member resource pertains to information about a person who is part of the deal registration team and who will be able to view the deal registration record. This resource can be automated by Magic xpi to help create deal team members (POST), delete deal team members (DELETE), list and retrieve deal team members (GET) and update a previously posted deal team member (PATCH).

**Deal Registration Notes.** In Oracle Sales Cloud, a Deal Registration Note resource records information such as comments, descriptive information, or special instructions related to a registered deal. A note is a record attached to a business object. Notes capture nonstandard information received as you do business, especially unstructured text. Magic xpi can automatically create (POST), delete (DELETE), get a list (GET), retrieve an individual note (GET), or update (PATCH) data that is pertaining to a Deal Registration Note.

**Deal Registration Opportunities.** The deal registration process does not create opportunities; it registers them to a deal. The deal registration opportunity resource is used to list and view the opportunities associated with a deal registration. As described in Chapter 7, an opportunity record allows a sales organization to track information about a specific potential sale including the sales account, key contacts, product interests, and potential revenues. When checking for duplicate deals, a "matched opportunity" is one that matches the deal registration based on the duplicate check process. Magic xpi can automatically get a list (GET) of or retrieve an individual deal registration opportunity (GET).

**Deal Registration Product Groups.** As discussed in Chapter Ten, Oracle Sales Cloud products have a complex data structure. In Oracle Sales Cloud, the deal registration product group resource controls product group information related to a registered deal. A product group is a business object that associates related products to one another, so that the users can handle them together. Product groups become the building blocks for organizing your sales catalog, a rollup hierarchy, or a promotion catalog. For example, you might create a product group named Audio Products that includes all of your audio products so that customers can browse through all the products in this group in your product catalog. Magic xpi can automatically get a list (GET) of or retrieve an individual deal registration product group (GET).

**Deal Registration Products.** In Oracle Sales Cloud, the deal registration product resource controls product information related to a registered deal. A product is a business object that contains the item information for a good or service that your organization wants to sell. Products Magic xpi can automatically get a list (GET) of or retrieve an individual deal registration product group (GET).

# 15 INTEGRATION WITH ORACLE SALES CLOUD SALES MANAGEMENT FUNCTIONS

Some of the functions in **Oracle Sales Cloud** are rather unique to sales managers. Keeping the territories, source codes and competitor information can be cumbersome. To the extent possible, you will want to use **Magic xpi Integration Platform** to automate these functions and save sales managers and salespeople from the time and trouble of maintaining and aligning this data across multiple systems where it has relevance.

| Oracle Sales Cloud REST API: Sales Management Resources |
| --- |
| Source Codes |
| Competitors |
| Sales Promotions |

Table 15:Sales Management Resources

**Source Codes.** Assessing the effectiveness of marketing and sales efforts requires an awareness of campaigns and lead sources. Oracle Sales Cloud keeps track of Campaign Names, Campaign IDs, Source Codes, Source Code IDs, Campaign Types and whether the Source Code is Active. It also records metadata such as the creator of the source code and the date and time of its creation, last update, creator, and last updater. Magic xpi automates the Oracle Sales Cloud by executing the retrieval of a source code or list of source codes.

In Oracle Sales Cloud, a *source code* is a resource used to track lead generation and responses by each marketing campaign. Source Codes help gauge sales and marketing effectiveness of each campaign. Oracle Sales

Cloud uses the marketing source code as a unique identifier to represent a marketing campaign and its underlying execution. Magic xpi can automate the listing (GET) and retrieval (GET) of Source Codes in Oracle Sales Cloud.

**Competitors.** An organizations selling effectiveness cannot be understood fully without an appreciation for the competitive situation and environment. Tracking competitor information in Oracle Sales Cloud allows a sales organization to compete more effectively and learn from past competitive sales situations.

In Oracle Sales Cloud, the competitor resource allows you to see competitor details. In business, a competitor is a company in the same industry or a similar industry which offers a similar product or service that can reasonably be offered as a substitute for your own company's products or services. When selling, the activity of one or more competitors can reduce the price of goods and increase the number of "deal sweeteners" and financial incentives offered. Competitors compete for individual sales as well as overall market position, market awareness and market share.

In Oracle Sales Cloud, the competitor object stores competitor attributes including the SWOT analysis, and various nested items such as competitor product offering, how they map to the deploying organization's products, win/loss reasons, competitive literature and so on. Magic xpi can automate the listing (GET) and retrieval (GET) of Competitors in Oracle Sales Cloud.

**Sales Promotion.** In Oracle Sales Cloud, a sales promotion business object contains special pricing and offerings for customers. Magic xpi can automate the creation (POST), deletion (DELETE), listing (GET), retrieval (GET), and updating (PATCH) of Sales Promotions.

# 16 INTEGRATION WITH ORACLE SALES CLOUD SALES TERRITORIES

In Oracle Sales Cloud, a sales territories resource represents the relevant sales territory for a given user. A territory may be defined separately or in combination by geography, by vertical market, by products sold, by named accounts and any other criteria deemed relevant. In fact, Oracle Sales Cloud Sales Territories can be created based on several criteria such as postal code, area code, country, vertical market, size of company, product expertise, and geographical location.

| Oracle Sales Cloud REST API: Sales Territories Resources |
|---|
| Sales Territories |
|   Line of Business |
|   Resources |
|   Rules |
|     Rule Boundaries |
|     Rule Boundary Values |
| Table 16:Sales Territories Resources |

**Sales Territories.** A sales territory defines the work assignment of a sales resource (team member or team). It defines the jurisdiction that salespeople have over sales accounts, or the jurisdiction that channel sales managers have over partners and partner transactions.

**Line of Business.** When managing sales territories in Oracle Sales Cloud, the line of business resource is used to see the lines of business designated to a sales territory. Magic xpi can automate the listing (GET) and retrieval (GET) of the Sales Territories Line of Business in Oracle Sales Cloud.

**Resources.** A sales territories Resource attribute is used to designate the sales people designated to a specific territory. These are the team members that can view the information for leads, contacts, accounts, etc. in that territory. Magic xpi can automate the listing (GET) and retrieval (GET) of Sales Territories Resources in Oracle Sales Cloud.

**Rules.** In addition, Oracle Sales Cloud uses the Rules resource to view the territory rules (in essence, the coverage area) associated with a sales territory. Magic xpi can automate the listing (GET) and retrieval (GET) of Sales Territories Rules in Oracle Sales Cloud.

**Rule Boundaries.** Finally, in Oracle Sales Cloud the rule boundaries resource is used to view the rule boundaries (in essence, the coverage definition) and rule boundary values associated with a sales territory. Magic xpi can automate the listing (GET) and retrieval (GET) of Sales Territories Rule Boundaries and rule boundary values in Oracle Sales Cloud.

# 17 INTEGRATION WITH ORACLE SALES CLOUD SERVICE REQUESTS AND CATEGORIES

 As CRM Systems emerged in the late 1990s and early 2000s, a great deal of emphasis was placed on the concept that CRM incorporated three primary disciplines: marketing, sales and service. Only when information and processes regarding these three disciplines were centralized, so the CRM theorists opined, could one obtain a 360-degree view of the customer. In practice, early CRM systems were largely designed around sales automation features and specialized best-of-breed marketing and service systems emerged around the centralized CRM systems.

| Oracle Sales Cloud REST API: Service Requests and Categories Resources |
|---|
| Service Requests |
|   Attachments |
|   Channel Communications |
|   Contact Members |
| Messages |
|   Attachments |
|   Channel Communications |
|   Resources |
|   Service Requests References |
| Categories |

Table 17: Service Requests and Categories Resources

In Oracle CX Cloud, these three disciplines are handled by separate Oracle Cloud Applications: Oracle Sales Cloud, Oracle Eloqua Marketing Cloud and Oracle Service Cloud. But there are common objects that exist in Oracle Sales Cloud to enable visibility into customer service information, even when that information may come from a service software solution other than Oracle Service Cloud. It is for this reason, that we find the Oracle Sales Cloud Service Request resource available in the Oracle Sales Cloud REST API.

Customer Service applications and Field Service Management (FSM) solutions are likely candidates for integration to Oracle Sales Cloud Service Request resources. While customer service applications tend to be used in a call center, Field Service Management applications are oriented to delivery of service outside of the call center (see *Hot Use Case: ServiceMax*) below.

**Service Request.** In Oracle Sales Cloud, a service request document is used to track a customer's request for service. Service requests have a definite beginning date and are considered resolved when the issue is closed. Magic xpi can automate the creation (POST), deletion (DELETE), listing (GET), retrieval (GET), and updating (PATCH) of Service Requests.

**Service Request Attachments.** In Oracle Sales Cloud, Service Request attachments are a list of files or URLs associated with a service request. Using Magic xpi, your developer or business analyst can automate the creation (POST), deletion (DELETE), listing (GET), retrieval (GET), and updating (PATCH) of Service Request Attachments.

**Channel Communications.** In Oracle Sales Cloud, channel communications comprise the data relating to recorded information exchanges between support agents and their customers. The system supports multi-channel communications including phone, email, SMS, Twitter and more. For example, the type of metadata recorded about communications includes the message id, recipient (contact) identifiers, and other various contact point identifiers. Magic xpi can automate the creation (POST), deletion (DELETE), listing (GET), retrieval (GET), and updating (PATCH) of Service Request Channel Communications.

**Contact Members.** In Oracle Sales Cloud, a Service Request Contact Members list contains the list of contacts that are associated to a Service Request. Customer service agents are in communication with Service Request Contact Members to resolve issues using a variety of communication channels. Magic xpi can automate the creation (POST), deletion (DELETE), listing (GET), retrieval (GET), and updating (PATCH) of Service Request Contact Members.

**Messages.** In Oracle Sales Cloud, service request messages contain unstructured message content and metadata for each iteration between the service agent and the customer as it pertains to a specific service request. A customer submit a request such as "I can't find the on switch" to the agent and the agent might respond "I'm sorry you are having difficulty, please refer to the diagram on p. 53 of the manual which shows the location of the on/off switch in the upper right panel." Message metadata includes the channel, date, time and other information regarding the message content. Using Magic xpi, your business analyst or developer can design processes that automate the creation (POST), deletion (DELETE), listing (GET), retrieval (GET), and updating (PATCH) of Service Request Message resources.

**Message Attachments.** In Oracle Sales Cloud, Service Request *message* attachments are a list of files or URLs associated with a service request message. Using Magic xpi, your developer or business analyst can automate the creation (POST), deletion (DELETE), listing (GET), retrieval (GET), and updating (PATCH) of Service Request Attachment Messages.

**Resource Members.** In Oracle Sales Cloud, Service Request *resource members* are the workforce members (employees or partners) that serve as service representatives, service managers, product managers and so on and who can take ownership of service request items, such as specific service requests, research requests, or knowledge base requests, in the service queue. Using Magic xpi, your developer or business analyst can automate the creation (POST), deletion (DELETE), listing (GET), retrieval (GET), and updating (PATCH) of Service Request Resource Members.

**References.** In Oracle Sales Cloud, the Service Request References resource contains the various knowledge items associated with a service request. These may be articles, reference links, previous service answers, and so on. The API is not used to update the reference resources. Using Magic xpi, your developer or business analyst can automate the creation (POST), deletion (DELETE), listing (GET), and retrieval (GET) of Service Request References.

**Categories.** In Oracle Sales Cloud, the Categories Resource is also related to Services so we discuss it here. As the name implies, a category is a means of grouping related service objects for easier classification and reports. A good example of a service request category is installation service requests. Categories can be arranged around the idea as to the type of service requested (call center inquiry, on-site request, etc.) or the subject matter of the service offered such as transmission service, radiator service, and so on. Categories can also be used to classify knowledge articles by subject matter such as error codes, tips and tricks, performance tuning or manual overrides.

Using Magic xpi, your developer or business analyst can automate the creation (POST), deletion (DELETE), listing (GET), retrieval (GET), and updating (PATCH) of Categories of services offered.

Hot Use Case: ServiceMax Field Service Management

ServiceMax, from GE Digital, is an increasingly popular Field Service Management solution that focuses on service outcomes. In 2016, GE Digital acquired ServiceMax and they emerged as the leader in the Gartner Quadrant for Field Service Management. ServiceMax is built on the Force.com platform, but that does not mean that it may only be used with Salesforce.com. Magic xpi Integration Platform can help integrate ServiceMax with Oracle Sales Cloud and your Enterprise Resource Planning (ERP) system as well. Westmor Industries is a good example of a company that has fully integrated ServiceMax. The business reasons for improving the integration to your Field Service Management (FSM) solution are manifold. A recent article in Baseline Magazine by Bobby Culbertson of Westmor mentions that after integrating ServiceMax, they saw an increase in Field Service Engineer (FSE) Utilization Gains when billable hours increased from 30-35% per field service technician to 60-65%. Integration with CRM and ERP can help you get the full value of your investment in ServiceMax in a number of key areas:

**Increase in FTF Rates.** Integration improves First Time Fix rates by ensuring information contained in enterprise systems doesn't get trapped there: vehicle inventory, purchase histories, and other legacy data can be critical to making sure you increase FTF rates.

**Reduction in MTTR.** Mean-time-to-repair is an important field service metric. Better integration between systems helps to ensure that automatic triggers and event handlers are in place for improved dispatching, route optimization and service productivity.

**Increase in NPS.** Businesses with a high Net Promoter Score (NPS) tend to thrive and grow while brands with a low NPS are industry laggards. Better integration enhances the customer experience leading to an increase in NPS. Better visibility of customer information, legacy data and faster triggering of processes all lead to an improved quality and efficiency of service, better up-sell/cross-sell and increased uptime.

# 18 INTEGRATION WITH ORACLE SALES CLOUD PAYMENTS AND PAYSHEETS

Payment of commissions is an important **CRM** feature that is not always well implemented in other sales automation and CRM systems. **Oracle Sales Cloud** has all the features you need to administer incentive compensation. And the **Oracle Sales Cloud REST API** provides **Magic xpi Integration Platform** with the ability to automate business processes related to incentive compensation for your Salesforce.

| Oracle Sales Cloud REST API: Payments and Paysheets  Resources |
| :--- |
| Payment Batches |
|   Payment Transactions |
|   Paysheets |
|    Payment Transactions |
| Payment Transactions |
| Paysheets |
|   Payment Transactions |
| Table 18: Payments and Paysheets Resources |

Oracle Sales Cloud provides the ability to manage incentive compensation and payments. In Oracle Sales Cloud, the Payments, Paysheets and Payment Batches are highly interrelated resources that provide for business process automation around incentive compensation. Payment Transactions can be a child resource of either Payment Batches or Paysheets. Paysheets may also be a child resource of Payment Batches. So a payment transaction resource can be called at a primary, secondary or tertiary level.

**Payment Batches.** In Oracle Sales Cloud, an API resource called the *payment batch* resource can be called to retrieve summary data related to payment batches. It can also be used to call and display the specific details of the paysheets and individual payment transactions contained in a particular payment batch. The payment batch will generate the paysheets for each of the employees receiving incentive compensation payments if they meet a payment batch generates paysheets for each incentive compensation participant if they meet the payment batch selection criteria. A paysheet is similar to a paystub in that it holds and displays the payment transaction amount. A payment transaction is basically the sales commission and other bonus incentives owed including any payment plan sales draws and recoverable or non-recoverable draw amounts, and also makes provision for any override adjustments to the payable amount.

With Magic xpi Integration Platform, your business analyst or developer can automatically retrieve a specific payment batch (GET) or retrieve a list of payment batches (GET).

**Payment Batches Payment Transactions.** Within the context of a payment batch, the payment transaction resource is used available to retrieve, create, and update participant payment transactions within the context of a payment batch. A payment transaction can be the calculated earnings from an incentive compensation plan component, a manual adjustment, a recovered amount, or a payment plan draw and recovery adjustment. The payment batch, payment transaction resource is also used to manage payment transaction holds and to create manual adjustments.

With Magic xpi Integration Platform, your business analyst or developer can automatically create (POST) a payment transaction, retrieve a specific payment transaction (GET) or retrieve a list of payment transactions (GET) or update a payment transaction (PATCH).

**Payment Batches Paysheets.** In Oracle Sales Cloud, when working with payment batches you can use the paysheet resource. A payment batch automatically creates paysheets for each person who should receive incentive compensation according to the the payment batch selection criteria. On the paysheet itself, you will find the specific payment transaction for the participant for the specified pay period. The resource also provides summarized amounts, such as total calculated earnings, total recoverable payment plan adjustments, and total payment amount.

With Magic xpi Integration Platform, your business analyst or developer can automatically retrieve a specific payment batch paysheet (GET) or retrieve a list of payment batch paysheets (GET).

**Payment Batches Paysheets Payment Transactions.** In Oracle Sales Cloud, within the context of a Payment Batch Paysheet, the payment transaction resource of the API is used to retrieve, create, and update participant payment transactions. The payment transactions can be based on the automatically calculated earnings from an incentive compensation plan component, a manual incentive compensation adjustment, a recovered incentive amount, or a payment plan draw and draw recovery adjustment. The payment batch paysheet payment transaction resource can also manage payment transaction holds and post adjustments manually.

With Magic xpi Integration Platform, your business analyst or developer can automatically create (POST) a payment batch paysheet payment transaction, retrieve a specific payment transaction (GET) or retrieve a list of payment transactions (GET) or update a payment transaction (PATCH).

**Payment Transactions.** In Oracle Sales Cloud, the payment transaction resource is used to retrieve participant payment transactions. A payment transaction can be the calculated earnings from an incentive compensation plan component, a manual adjustment, a recovered amount, or a payment plan draw and recovery adjustment. The payment transaction resource is also used to manage payment transaction holds and to create manual adjustments.

With Magic xpi Integration Platform, your business analyst or developer can automatically create (POST) a payment transaction, retrieve a specific payment transaction (GET) or retrieve a list of payment transactions (GET) or update a payment transaction (PATCH).

**Paysheets.** In Oracle Sales Cloud, the paysheet resource allows you to retrieve the paysheet information. As noted, a payment batch generates a paysheet for each incentive compensation participant according to the payment batch criteria that has been set. On the paysheet itself, you will find the specific payment transaction for the participant for the specified pay period. You can view summarized amounts including total calculated earnings, total recoverable payment plan adjustments, and total payment amount.

With Magic xpi Integration Platform, your business analyst or developer can automatically retrieve a specific paysheet (GET) or retrieve a list of paysheets (GET).

**Paysheet Payment Transactions.** In Oracle Sales Cloud, the paysheet payment transaction resource is used to view, create, and update participant payment transactions as indicated by the paysheet. The specific payment transaction can be calculated automatically as earnings based on the paysheet details for the incentive compensation plan component or posted as a manual adjustment, a recovered amount, or a payment plan draw and recovery adjustment. You can also use the payment transaction resource to set payment transaction holds or make manual adjustments.

With Magic xpi Integration Platform, you can automatically create (POST) a paysheet payment transaction, retrieve a specific paysheet payment transaction (GET) or retrieve a list of paysheet payment transactions (GET) or update a paysheet payment transaction (PATCH).

# 19 INTEGRATION WITH ORACLE SALES CLOUD RESOURCES AND QUEUES

Like many **CRM** systems, you will want to call on needed resources and interact with specific queues in **Oracle Sales Cloud** as well. The **Oracle Sales Cloud REST API** can be accessed by **Magic xpi Integration Platform** to manipulate the use of **Queues and Resources** in Oracle Sales Cloud.

| Oracle Sales Cloud REST API: Queues and Resources *Resources* |
| --- |
| Queues |
|     Queue Resource Members |
|     Queue Resource Teams |
| Resources |
|     Attachments |
| Table 19: Queues and Resources *Resources* |

**Queues.** In Oracle Sales Cloud, a *Queue* is an array of open requests pending assignment to a service team member. Keep in mind that, team members can use the application to select requests to work on or they may assign a request to a desired team member. A good examples of the use of queues would be territory queues such as South America Queue or product lines such as Luxury Lines Queue. With Magic xpi Integration Platform, your business analyst or developer can automatically create (POST) a queue, retrieve a specific queue (GET), retrieve a list of all queues (GET), delete a queue (DELETE) or update a queue (PATCH).

**Queue Resources Members.** In Oracle Sales Cloud, a Queue *Resource Member* may contain members in a list of employees or partners available or assigned to act as a resource in the CRM process. These may be customer service representatives (CSR), service managers (SM), or product managers (PM), who can take responsibility for tasks and be assigned as a resource for activities such as service request or a knowledge authoring task that may be lined up in the queue.

With Magic xpi Integration Platform, your business analyst or developer can automatically create (POST) a queue resource member, delete a queue resource member (DELETE), retrieve a specific queue resource member (GET), retrieve a list of all queue resource members (GET), or update a queue resource member (PATCH).

**Queue Resources Teams.** In Oracle Sales Cloud, a Queue *Resource Team* contains a team or list of members assigned to a queue. A team is an established list of employees or partners available or assigned to act as a resource in the CRM process. A team may be composed of a single discipline such as CSRs or may be a cross disciplinary team comprised of individual CSRs, PMs, SMs etc. who are available for task assignments. Teams may also represent geographies or even arbitrary collections of members.

With Magic xpi Integration Platform, your business analyst or developer can automatically create (POST) a queue resource team, delete a queue resource team (DELETE), retrieve a specific queue resource team (GET), retrieve a list of all queue resource teams (GET), or update a queue resource team (PATCH).

**Resources.**

Not all resources are assigned through queues, however. In Oracle Sales Cloud, resources may be managed individually.

**Resources.** In Oracle Sales Cloud, the *Resources* resource is used to view a resource. According to Oracle Sales Cloud terminology, a resource is a "person within the deploying company who can be assigned work to accomplish business objectives, such as sales persons or partner members."

With Magic xpi Integration Platform, your business analyst or developer can automatically retrieve a specific resource (GET) or retrieve a list of resources (GET).

**Resource Attachments.** One of the best ways to identify someone is by their picture. For this reason, Oracle Sales Cloud provides an attachment capability to a resource which contains an image file or picture. In Oracle Sales Cloud, the contact picture Resource *Attachment* resource is used to view resource pictures.

With Magic xpi Integration Platform, your business analyst or developer can automatically retrieve a specific resource attachment, or picture (GET) or retrieve a list of resource attachments or pictures (GET).

# 20 TERMINOLOGY AND USE CASE SCENARIOS

 Up until this point, we have focused on what the Magic xpi Integration Platform can do with the Oracle Sales Cloud REST API, now we will begin to focus on how you can invoke any of these API capabilities using Magic xpi. To have that discussion, we need to define some terms. When discussing the integration of information technology systems, a variety of terms that can be classified as industry jargon are commonly used. In addition, each integration middleware product tends to use its own nomenclature to describe its features and functions. At times, the internal nomenclature of the application matches the most common use of the term in industry jargon; however, it is very common for the use of a particular term to have specific meaning within a particular middleware or integration tool or platform. For this reason, it is useful to establish some basic terminology before heading into specific discussion of the Magic xpi Integration Platform and how it accomplishes the specific capabilities outlined in the previous chapters. These terms are being defined in the context of business systems integration.

**Application.** An application is a software program that is used to accomplish business tasks.

**Data.** Data is the structured and unstructured information generated, viewed or managed by your business applications. Structured data is usually stored in SQL databases. Unstructured information is frequently transported and stored in XML format; however both SQL and XML are capable of dealing with structured and unstructured data.

**ETL.** Extract, Transform and Load. A type of middleware focused on data integration that reads data from a source application's dataset, converts it to the format of another application if needed, and stores that transformed data with the target application's dataset, usually a structured SQL database.

**ESB.** Enterprise Service Bus. An on demand middleware layer that facilitates message exchange between applications. Messages often contain data used in applications.

**EAI.** Enterprise Application Integration. A middleware approach focused on interacting with application functionality and transforming data.

**BPM.** Business Process Management. An integration approach that listens to application activity, triggers application functionality, and facilitates inter-application business steps and workflow independently of the applications themselves. Forrester Research categorizes BPM as IC-BPMS (Integration Centric Business Process Management Systems) and HC-BPMS (Human Centric Business Process Management Systems.)

**Event Driven Architecture.** An approach in software that triggers logical steps based on system, application and user events.

**SOA.** Service Oriented Architecture. An approach to software design that emphasizes the use of reusable units of business logic available to be found, called, discovered and executed by independent units or applications.

**WEB Services.** Internet based functions that allow for remote publish and subscribe activities.

**SOAP.** Structured Object Access Protocol. A highly defined Web Service protocol based on XML often used with WSDL and UDDI to provide SOA capabilities.

**WSDL.** Web Services Description Language. The details of the syntax, functionality and structure of a SOAP Web Service also based on XML.

**UDDI.** Universal Description, Discovery and Integration. An XML format for publishing descriptions of web services that can be found over the Web.

**Adapters.** Sometimes called components or endpoint adapters, an adapter is a middleware software unit designed to work with a specific application, for example an Oracle E-Business Suite (EBS) adapter or a Microsoft Exchange Email Server adapter.

**API.** Application Programming Interface. Any of a variety of methods provided by a software program to enable interchange. APIs tend to be one of three types: complex application function APIs, data import and export APIs, and user interface or mashup APIs.

In addition to these general industry terms for middleware, it is useful to consider some usages that have specific meaning when using Magic xpi Integration Platform.

**Project.** A related group of business processes and flows used to accomplish a business process integration activity.

**Business Process.** A related group of flows.

**Flow.** A series of steps and logical branches in a Magic xpi process. The basic procedures or routines used in your integration project with Magic xpi.

**Data Mapper.** The drag and drop interface that allows Magic xpi to move information to and from source and destination while applying logical expressions in the expression editor needed to reformat the information to the applications desired schema.

**Expression Editor.** A powerful single line notation of business logic using a full set of arithmetic, string and logical functions and operators. Used in the Data Mapper and other situations.

**Components.** The adapters used to create steps in a Magic xpi flow. A good example would be the JD Edwards EnterpriseOne component.

**Resources.** A variety of sources for use in a Magic xpi flow. A database such as an Oracle database can be invoked as a source in a Magic xpi flow.

**Methods.** A variety of procedures to be used to apply functional business logic in a Magic xpi flow.

**Errors.** Magic xpi tracks program exceptions or errors using flow error policies, error messages and an errors repository. You can see specific errors in the monitor logs and error summaries in the dashboards.

**Synchronous.** A step in a Magic xpi Integration flow that keeps an open thread for a response to the interaction, such as a synchronous message with a Message Queue (MSMQ, JMS, MQ-Series).

**Asynchronous.** A step in a Magic xpi Integration flow that does not wait for an immediate response and does not keep an open thread. Examples of asynchronous steps include scheduled activities and near real-time steps in a Web Service API.


**Use Cases.** A use case provides an example of a common business process integration requirement for Oracle Sales Cloud users. Oracle Sales Cloud can be integrated with a wide variety of applications. Among the most common applications needing integration to Oracle Sales Cloud:

- **ERP.** Enterprise Resource Planning. ERP applications manage the accounting, finances, planning and related business functions of a company. Popular ERP systems to which Oracle Sales Cloud may need to integrate include: Oracle ERP Cloud, Oracle E-Business Suite, Oracle JD Edwards, Oracle PeopleSoft Enterprise, NetSuite, SAP ERP, SAP Business One, Microsoft Dynamics ERP (AX/GP/NAV/SL), Infor, Sage, and Syspro.

- **eCommerce Platforms.** An eCommerce platform places your company store or webshop online and receives orders for goods and services. In order for your sales team to have visibility into customer orders online, you need integration between Oracle Sales Cloud and your eCommerce platforms. There are hundreds of different eCommerce platforms including Oracle Commerce Cloud, Oracle Commerce (on-premise), IBM WebSphere Commerce, Jaguar, Magento, Shopatron and many others.

- **PLM.** Product Lifecycle Management. PLM systems manage the data and business processes from end-to-end for your company's goods and services. The product lifecycle includes research, ideation, design, prototyping, testing, scaling, tooling, assembling, manufacturing, supplying, distributing, servicing, changing, downsizing, retrofitting, refurbishing, repairing, recycling and discontinuing of products. Oracle Sales Cloud users commonly need to see PLM Work Orders and their information. Common PLM systems include Oracle Cloud PLM, Oracle Agile PLM, Siemens Teamcenter, DS3, Windchill and Selerant.

- **SCM.** Supply Chain Management. As the name implies, SCM systems are concerned with organizing information and processes surrounding the various, often interconnected, resources and inputs needed to produce goods and services. The sales forecast data produced by Oracle Sales Cloud is an essential input to a company's SCM systems for demand forecasting and manufacturing planning and scheduling purposes. Oracle Sales Cloud may need to integrate with any of a variety of SCM systems including Oracle SCM Cloud, Demantra, JDA Software, Blue Ridge, Kinaxis, OM Partners, ToolsGroup, GAINSystems, Steelwedge, Quintiq, SAS, and Logility.

- **Logistics Systems.** A wide variety of types of logistics systems exist in the market today. Sales people are often called upon to answer three important logistics questions: when will I get my stuff, how much will it cost to (ship) get my stuff and once the order is placed: "Where's my stuff!?" Integration of Oracle Sales Cloud to logistics systems is vital to providing the salesperson and ultimately the customer with an answer to these questions. Logistics systems include Transportation Management Systems, Warehouse Management Systems, 3PL software, and much more. In addition to full applications, many shippers provide Web Services for tracking and accounting for logistics. All of these can have relevance and importance to Oracle Sales Cloud users.

- **Marketing Automation Systems.** Within the Oracle CX Cloud, Oracle Sales Cloud and Eloqua have several strictly defined integration objects. Beyond the basics, however, an integration system is required to allow your business analyst to control specific integration processes for your business. Oracle Sales Cloud integration to marketing automation systems allows for several processes to occur: marketing handoff of leads to sales, sales visibility into marketing campaigns, marketing measurement of campaign effectiveness based on linked sales data, complete activity logs and 360-degree of customers, better segmentation and sales and marketing cycle awareness for both systems, return of leads to the marketing pool, measurable feedback on lead quality, better access and integration of sales and marketing document libraries, better social marketing and selling integration and more. Oracle Sales Cloud may need to integrate with any of a variety of marketing automation systems including Oracle Eloqua Cloud, Marketo, Hubspot, Act-on, Pardot and Adobe Campaign.

- **CSM and FSM.** Customer Service Management and Field Service Management. Integrating Oracle Sales Cloud is essential for both sales and service users of your business systems. In order to gain a 360-dgree view of customer information, users of both systems need to be able to see important data and activities recorded in the other system. Magic xpi Integration Platform enables integration of Oracle Sales Cloud with a variety of CSM and FSM applications.

- **Accounts Receivable Integration.** Accounts receivable integration with Oracle Sales Cloud is certainly one of the "hot button" needs in many organizations. The need for AR integration primarily relates to providing the sales team with an accurate current view of receivables.

- **Opportunity-to-Order Conversion.** To get to the invoice, of course, you have to first create a sales order. Magic xpi enables a variety of automated processes including opportunity-to-order conversion. JD Edwards World is great at processing orders, but it has no functionality related to opportunity management and sales leads. JD Edwards World tables impacted in sales order management will be the F4201 and F4211 via the P42011Z batch transaction process. CRM systems also inter-relate with the JD Edwards address book and the F0101Z transaction tables. Address book integration is facilitated with the use of a Z process, P0101Z and impacts the files F0101, F0301 and F0401.

Many organizations running EnterpriseOne choose to use a third party CRM solution rather than the somewhat limited CRM capabilities of JD Edwards EnterpriseOne. To facilitate this integration, Magic xpi works with either the Master Business Functions or the Universal Batch Engine (UBE) Z file process depending on the situation. With the EnterpriseOne Sales Order Master Business Functions, Magic xpi automates the interactions with F4211FSBeginDoc, F4211FSEditLine, and F4211FSEndDoc. If the UBE is preferred, it runs R40211Z to access tables F4201 and F4211. These are just examples of course, as Magic xpi can interface with any JDE business function or UBE.

- Human Capital Management.

JD Edwards payroll features do not do a good job of dealing with sales commissions. You can create pay types when you set up the system. So make sure you have a type for commissions. Pulling the data from the CRM system you will then be able to apply your business rules for commission calculations. For JD Edwards World systems, Magic xpi will use P06110Z to bring in sales commission on a batch basis to the F06116 timecard management table, thereby facilitating payment processing. For EnterpriseOne, Magic xpi can orchestrate the R05116Z11 UBE to integrate access and manipulate the F06116Z1 table. Magic xpi can also orchestrate interactions via the EnterpriseOne Time Entry Master Business Function.

- **Manufacturing Management.**

In this pillar, of course, we find the gem of product data management and one of my favorite subjects: Master Item Data. When running the P4101 process the F4101 can be involved, of course. But that is just the tip of the iceberg. For example, if you are running P4101 processing option 7, UDC 40/IC there are more than 50 tables impacted. So obviously, as a business analyst getting into this area of integration, you need to be very cautious. I recommend pulling only a limited set of information from ERP to CRM and not even considering the reverse. I can't really think of business reasons to pull data from CRM into a Master Item table or tables in ERP. And overloading the CRM system with all of the detail available in an ERP system seems unnecessary. But to be sure, some of the master item data can be a key to competitive advantage by providing the agility needed for smooth running business processes whereby CRM interactions get down to the product level detail needed. Automated integration and synchronization of this data is essential because a mismatch in data will lead to business process errors and exceptions. When triggering a JD Edwards EnterpriseOne Master Business Function such as a Sales Order based on an event in Salesforce.com, keep in mind that there are interdependent data relationships to corresponding Work Orders, for example. An EnterpriseOne business analyst is needed to guide you through these details.

- **Distribution Management.** Three key areas of distribution management are likely targets for CRM integration relationships as well: sales order, inventory and warehouse management. One of the important touchpoints will be found in the area of inventory management. Item availability is obviously a key concern and can be addressed by the P41201 process / F41201 table. Putting a Magic xpi process in place that makes available inventory data visible to a salesperson using a CRM system can provide a novel advantage to your sales team – a unique competitive advantage. As mentioned, sales orders are going to be a common touchpoint as well. For JD Edwards World, you will be using the JD Edwards World P42011Z batch transaction process to populate the F4201 and F4211 tables. In EnterpriseOne, the corresponding batch process is R40211Z and the same tables are used. As mentioned before Magic xpi automates the EnterpriseOne Sales Order Master Business Functions interactions with F4211FSBeginDoc, F4211FSEditLine, and F4211FSEndDoc. Creating sales order entry integration between CRM and ERP will reduce the need for sales administrators to spend time manually entering sales orders for which the CRM system already has all the required details. A number of business rules need to be considered before automating the opportunity to order conversion process that spans the chasm between CRM and ERP, but it can be done.

# 21 MAGIC XPI INTEGRATION PLATFORM: MAGIC XPI STUDIO

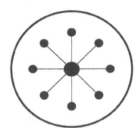

**Magic xpi Integration Platform** delivers enterprise-grade integration, business process automation, and data synchronization solutions for users of Oracle Sales Cloud and other enterprise software systems.

Someone with ambitions towards Oracle Sales Cloud integration using Magic xpi Integration Platform needs to learn the development principles and fundamental techniques of creating an integration project using Magic xpi, including testing, deploying, and maintaining the project in runtime. Prior to tackling such a project, you should already be familiar with database concepts such as tables, rows, fields, indexes and the relationships between these objects. In addition, you should take a refresher lesson on XML and related terms such as XSD, element, compound, and even namespaces. It is also very useful but not mandatory to already know something about SQL statements; HTML technology and tags; Web services concepts such as knowledge of REST APIs.

The next step in learning Magic xpi Integration Platform after moving beyond these prerequisites is to become familiar with the integration concepts, development environment, and components of Magic xpi.

Like other integration projects, Oracle Sales Cloud integration projects should follow a methodology in Magic xpi. You will need to learn how to approach the development of a Magic xpi project and appreciate the importance of following a standardized methodology to optimize the development process and then begin designing the integration in that project. This involves documenting the design of the project according to the business logic and the topology. Defining the topology is fairly simple as you are simply describing the world as it is. Defining the integration itself, is designing the world as it will become.

To do this, you will need to learn to populate the resource repository in the Solution Explorer which contains the various external sources for the project.

Once the project resources have been defined and arranged, the business processes in the project are to be defined next. It is now possible to actually begin writing the executable integration flows of a project.

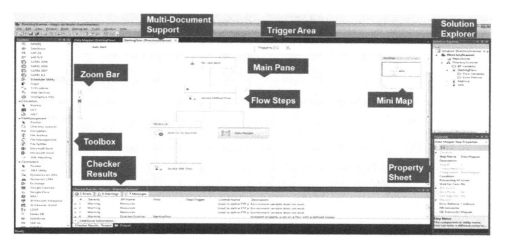

**Figure 21a.** Magic xpi Studio. Main flow created using drag, drop and configure approach to integration.

**Magic xpi Integration Studio** is typically used by business analysts, architects and developers to design business process flows for data and process integration. Magic updates the capabilities of the integration design studio from time-to-time. Sometimes these constitute a new major release of Magic Software's Magic xpi Integration Platform. New features and enhancements are designed to improve the user experience with a new look-and-feel as well as provide additional functionality for enterprise integration projects. The Magic xpi Integration Platform 4.6 utilizes the Magic xpa 3.1 Application Platform. All the necessary elements are included automatically at time of installation. You will need to select a database and have IIS (or equivalent) installed before using the Magic xpi Studio. To begin, let's examine the Magic xpi Studio which is a drag, drop and configure environment where you create integration flows between your enterprise applications.

Magic xpi Integration Platform provides a Visual Studio-based design studio offering an intuitive and user-friendly experience. Analysts, architects and developers who have used any other Microsoft Visual Studio product will find the shell and interface style of the Studio very familiar. The Magic xpi Studio offers a variety of capabilities, including:

**Docking capabilities.** Magic xpi's **workspace panes** show the most relevant information for your project in an easy to understand display. All the workspace panes have floating and docking capabilities, and can be resized simply by dragging their edges to the required size.

**MiniMap.** Magic xpi includes a MiniMap to enable you to navigate quickly within long or wide flows. Sometimes, a flow may be too long or have too many branches to be able to completely fit into the visible screen area. Magic xpi's MiniMap enables you to easily orient yourself within the flow and to quickly navigate to specific flow components.

**Toolbox Pane.** Magic xpi's Toolbox pane includes the Components and other tools you need to build integration process flows. The Toolbox pane is the first of the three main information panes in the Magic xpi Studio. The other two are the Solution Explorer and the Properties pane. When you select a flow in the Solution Explorer, the Toolbox pane is populated with a list of Magic xpi's components, grouped together under specific categories.

**Solution Explorer.** A Solution Explorer provides navigation capabilities. The Solution Explorer is the second of the three main information panes in the Magic xpi Studio. The Solution Explorer shows projects, repositories, business processes, and flows. When you click one of the entries, the main Properties pane shows the definitions for the selection.

**Properties.** The Properties pane is the third of the three main information panes in the Magic xpi Studio. It is a dedicated Properties pane that displays the properties of whichever part of the project that you are parked on. The Properties pane displays the properties of any configurable part of your project when you park on that specific element. For example, to make configuration changes to a specific component, you should park on that component in the main pane.

**Settings.** The Magic xpi Settings dialog box provides a central and easy-to-access location where you can manage the Resources, Services, Project Environment and General Environment of your project.

**Search.** A combined search functionality. The ability to find resource names and other text in your project is serviced by a Find Text dialog box.

**Copy and Paste.** The copy and paste mechanism supports multiple pasting of steps and branches.

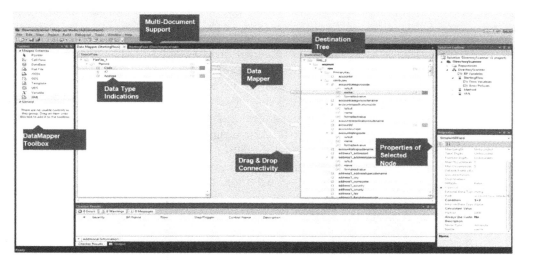

**Figure 21b.** The Magic xpi Studio Data Mapper allows for drag, drop and configure integration.

As you begin dragging and dropping components in the Studio, you will discover that the rapid design of a flow is quick and easy due to the ease-of-use provided by the Magic xpi Studio. Properties and Configuration are easily maintained in dialog boxes that are clean and easy-to-use.

**Figure 21c.** Data Mapper Window.

Magic xpi Studio is designed for business analysts, architects and developers to streamline business processes without writing code. Applications can be connected from the cloud or ground making this a hybrid integration tool. Processes can span diverse applications, platforms, and databases. Magic xpi provides the means to take control of your IT environments and integrate your business information, logic, and data into cross-organizational, cross-platform business processes. The purpose of creating smooth running business processes is to reduce operational costs, improve revenue performance, and reduce business risk.

The key to the way Magic xpi simplifies the design and integration process is a separation of business logic from the underlying integration technology. Magic xpi provides visual tools like wizards, drag-and-drop components, and data maps to create seamless connections with enterprise applications deployed on any hardware, operating system, or database technology.

Magic xpi Studio is a business process development environment and IDE. Magic xpi Studio offers two main interfaces: the Flow Editor and the Data Mapper. With these visual tools, business analysts can orchestrate business processes, define data transformations, and control message flow. Magic xpi also provides development and modeling aids that assist the business process developer in designing and implementing their solution. Let's look more in-depth at the Flow Editor.

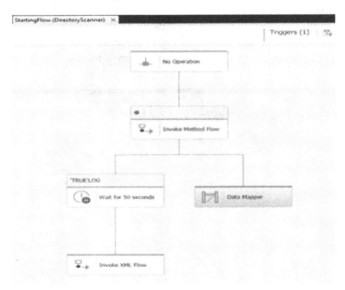

**Figure 21d.** This flow uses a trigger and includes a branch for conditional logic, a wait step, and a data mapping step.

With the Magic xpi Flow Editor, business process developers define the business processes that they want to exist between enterprise applications. Granular integration flows perform the work in Magic xpi. These flows establish all internal and external data manipulations to be performed as well as numerous means of message communication and transactions. The connectivity formed between business applications may be comprised of message exchange, data transformations, and surrounding business logic. A flow consists of visually inter-connected components such as connectors, adapters, converters, and logical controls that together provide overall business process functionality across users, applications, systems and environments. Flows define component relationships and the logic that defines how the Magic xpi Server will run the flow once the project is live.

An example of a simple flow could be reading an application business object such as a JD Edwards Business Function that references the F0101 table, selecting data from within it, converting it to XML, and transmitting it using REST Web Services to Oracle Sales Cloud as a lead, household, contact or account resource. Magic xpi flows can interact with one another in whole or in part and can access an Operational Data Store (ODS) that logs all transactions according to the flow designers' requirements.

The flow editor allows for visual flow definitions using a number of capabilities. The flow editor allows for definition of business rules and conditional logic, functions, expressions, branches, and control flow operations. Using the integration flow editor, flows can be triggered by events from any application including Oracle Sales Cloud, Oracle Eloqua, Oracle E-Business Suite and even third-party applications and websites. This gives Magic xpi built-in capabilities comparable to an enterprise service bus (ESB) and en event-driven architecture. In addition, Magic xpi flows can be scheduled to run in intervals, similar to an Extract, Transform and Load (ETL) tool with control based on a calendar, on startup or continuously. Unlike an ETL or ESB, all flows may in addition be transactional, meaning they provide integrated recovery and error handling mechanisms. Complex business process management (BPM) capabilities are thereby enabled as flow logic can be split into multiple, parallel running processes. Outside the Magic xpi Studio at runtime, these flows are managed and monitored by an IT administrator using Magic xpi's integrated monitoring and logging tools. We'll look at those in the next chapter.

# 22 MAGIC XPI INTEGRATION PLATFORM: MAGIC XPI MONITOR

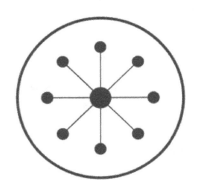

The Magic xpi Integration Platform server does not have a user interface on its own. It runs silently in the background connecting all your application processes, logic and data from *Oracle Sales Cloud* to any other CRM, ERP, PLM, eCommerce, logistics and other applications including all of the apps in the Oracle CX Cloud. So while all this integration is running on an unseen server, Magic provides a Magic Monitor that looks in on your projects and provides complete visibility of what is taking place.

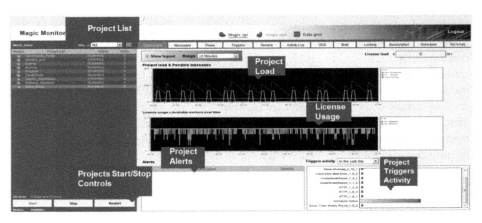

**Figure 22.** Magic Monitor. Shows the project work load over time.

As such, one of the most visible elements of Magic xpi Integration Platform is the Magic Monitor. Sometimes, even when the integration seems *like Magic* you want to see behind the curtain. The Magic Monitor let's you do just that. Let's take a look at the monitor and its role in integration. It is important to note that the Monitor has been designed to serve both the Magic xpi Integration Platform and the Magic xpa Application Platform infrastructure. The purpose of the monitor is to give you accurate information about your integration projects and Magic applications from a unified and intuitive dashboard that is easy to use. You can tab between the Magic xpi dashboard, the Magic xpa dashboard and the Data Grid Dashboard.

This information in the Magic xpi Dashboard allows you to manage your integration project, alert you to any problems, and maintain the project to optimize performance. Looking at data loads, for example, you can identify potential performance issues and you can also monitor license usage within a project to prevent bottlenecks in case of a shortage.

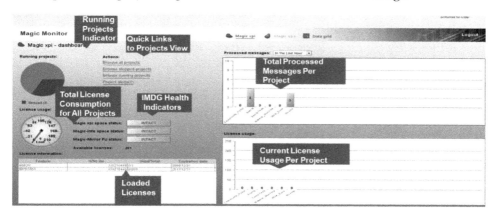

**Figure 22b.** Magic Monitor. Dashboard shows IMDG Infrastructure.

The Magic Monitor allows you to see information about a whole project or levels within a project. Information is updated and displayed to show the current situation. Using filters you can view integration flow project results for specific time frames. The Magic Monitor looks into each Space within a project and reports its status.

The alerts from the Magic Monitor can be communicated in real-time. If the status of a space is broken or compromised, for example, you can receive an alert. When an alternate license is being utilized, an alert can be triggered as well so that you can take appropriate actions. You can also browse all projects, running projects, stopped projects and review alerts from the dashboard. The dashboard displays the projects you have running, license usage, status of in-memory spaces, license info, usage and availability, and the volume of messages processed in a project.

The Data Grid Dashboard shows the status of an in-memory data grid space, the distribution of space partitions, and space-related alerts. You can see the grid hosts (essentially the servers providing memory and processing to the spaces) and their IP addresses, CPU utilization, and memory utilization.

You can also get detailed information about the grid components and Magic engines. The monitoring capabilities of the Magic xpi Integration Platform also include the ability to create flow and component logs. Log files can be inspected to review the step-by-step information that you choose. Combined together, the monitoring and logging capabilities of Magic xpi Integration Platform gives you the ability to manage and maintain the details of your Magic environment, projects, in-memory data grids, spaces, flows and components.

# 23 MAGIC XPI INTEGRATION PLATFORM: MAGIC XPI SERVER

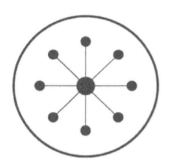

**Magic xpi Integration Platform Server** architecture can be defined by describing several of its constituent elements. These are not so much physical units as they are abstractions that define the interaction of the various software layers in the Magic xpi Integration Platform.

**In-Memory Data Grid (IMDG).** When the server is executing a project, it needs access to storage. Whereas traditional computing systems store information in databases on physical hard drives, Magic uses an *In Memory Computing* approach. The Magic xpi **in-memory data grid** is middleware software composed of multiple server processes running on multiple machine instances (physical or virtual) that work together to store large amounts of data in memory, thereby achieving high performance, elastic scalability, and fail-safe redundancy. Magic xpi Integration Platform uses the In-Memory Data Grid to host *Spaces*.

**Space.** A *Space* is a data and business logic container (similar to a database instance) running in the data grid. A data grid can contain multiple Spaces. Magic xpi 4.5 uses two main Spaces, and a third Space for mirroring to the database, for running multiple projects. For redundancy and scalability, data and business logic in the Spaces are replicated and partitioned across all machines participating in the data grid, ensuring continuous service even in case of machine or software failure.

**Magic Processing Unit (PU).** In order to properly manage the execution of integration projects in the *Spaces* on the *In Memory Data Grid,*

Magic xpi utilizes a software capability called the **Magic Processing Unit** or (PU). The *Magic PU* is a software module that runs in the Space and performs various management tasks on the project objects. This PU monitors and manages all Magic xpi objects and makes sure the server is running properly. The Magic PU has a number of management functions, including:

- Identifying flow timeout situations and recovering from them;

- Identifying hung or crashed *workers* (see below) and servers and recovering from them;

- Distributing management messages to running servers;

- Clearing completed flow requests;

- Gathering statistics on project entities.

The various PUs can be seen in the GigaSpaces UI, under Event Containers. There is additional information in the GigaSpaces UI which can be useful. For example, the Processed column provides details about the number of requests that were processed in each PU, and how many timeouts occurred. There are two dedicated PUs (one PU for the HTTP trigger type, named **http2ifr**, and one PU for all others, named **externalRequestToFlowRequest**. These names are used in the Space that converts these Temp msgs into FlowRequest messages and can be seen in the Event Containers section of the GigaSpaces UI. These FlowRequest messages are handled by the Magic xpi Server.

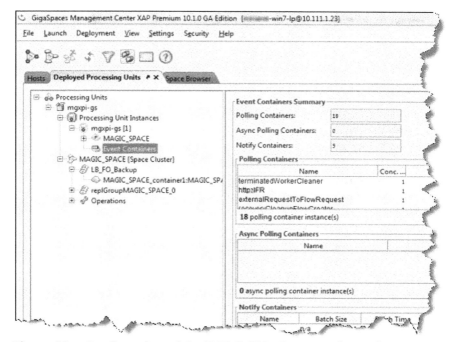

**Figure 23a.** Configuration of the IMDG PUs, Spaces and containers.

**Magic xpi Server.** The Magic xpi Server is the engine that runs your integration project during deployment. Magic xpi Servers use the information contained in the ibp file that you generated in the Magic xpi Studio to run the project. Magic xpi Servers contain various systems that manage the different aspects of flow execution.

Magic xpi Servers contain a set of systems that provide a range of flow-management services, such as messaging. The Servers also provide logging and monitoring functionality that help you carry out performance modifications and enhancements.

The **Flow Manager** is the main Server module that manages flow invocation and ongoing flow execution.

The **Publish and Subscribe** (PSS), **Operational Data Store** (ODS), **Locking and Messaging** (MSG) systems are used for data management and storage in the project. The PSS and the Locking system are handled in the Space, while the Messaging system and the ODS are handled in the database. The **Recovery** system is used for recovery operations. The **Scheduler** system manages the timing of flow execution.

**Triggers.** Magic xpi is designed to respond to real-time events using a variety of triggers. Triggers may arrive via a variety of methods including Web Servers such as **IIS, Tomcat** and **Systinet.**

*Push Triggers.* A request for Magic xpi that arrives from push triggers is handled by a Magic class called Mgrequest which alerts the Magic xpi server process by putting a Temp FlowRequest msg into the Space. This is unlike a WS/HTTP trigger handled by the Web Server which handles the request in a separate process.

*Polling Triggers.* All other requests that invoke a trigger are handled inside a Magic xpi server process (that does not utilize Mgrequest) which directly writes FlowRequest messages to the Space. Available workers in the Space take FlowRequest messages and execute them, taking into account the project's constraints (max instances, licenses, and so on).

**Flow Workers.** Flow workers are capable of executing process logic in your flow and are also referred to as threads; that is, a processing thread that can execute flows. A flow worker performs flow steps. Flow workers start and wait for flow invocation requests which are messages looking for flow workers whose status in the Space is READY_FOR_USE. Once a flow invocation request message is being handled, the flow worker changes its status in the Space to IN_PROCESS. It does this within a transaction to prevent two workers from executing the same message, and runs the requested flow defined in the message using the data available in the message payload.

The flow worker maintains detailed status information in the Space during its operation to enable detailed monitoring, troubleshooting, and maintenance. Before running each step in the flow, the worker updates the Space with the current flow status and then, according to the project metadata, it checks if it needs to:

- Abort due to reaching its user defined timeout;

- Abort due to recovery or error handling;

- Abort due to server/project shutdown;

- Pause before continuing to the next step (in debug state).

When the flow is complete, the worker updates the flow invocation request message's status in the Space to DONE, and starts waiting for additional new messages to handle.

Magic xpi prioritizes messages with a higher depth when reading messages from the Space, ensuring that a business process is completed before a new one starts.

The processing strategy for root messages is first in first out (FIFO), but messages which are deeper in the execution tree (parallel steps) have a higher priority and will be processed before any waiting root messages. This strategy allows for the quicker completion of execution trees before a new root message is handled.

**Trigger Workers.** These are threads that are responsible for polling or "listening" to external events and initiating flows by creating flow invocation requests in the Space. Trigger threads start and wait for external events to occur. Once such an event occurs, the trigger creates a flow invocation request (message) with the event data (payload), to be handled by available flow workers. Triggers can be synchronous or asynchronous.

**Synchronous Triggers:** While some triggers invoke flow requests asynchronously, other triggers have a synchronous working mode. In synchronous mode, after the trigger creates an invoke flow request, it will wait for a response message. The flow worker that handles a synchronous request is responsible for creating the response message with the payload once the flow is complete.

**Asynchronous Triggers:** These triggers create flow request messages and immediately continue to check for new events in the external system, without waiting for a response. To prevent asynchronous triggers from flooding the Space with unhandled flow request messages, each trigger has a predefined queue buffer size that will be used to throttle the creation of new events if the queue exceeds the predefined size. This trigger buffer size has a default value of 10. You can adjust this value by changing the trigger buffer flag value. Just like flow workers, triggers maintain their state in the Space, to ensure maintainability and visibility.

**Project Execution Sequence.**

1. **Running the task.** When the project is running, three elements operate simultaneously: workers, polling triggers, and external triggers. Each Magic xpi server can run one or more workers or triggers for a variety of tasks.

*Polling Triggers.* A polling trigger (such as the Directory Scanner), also known as an asynchronous trigger, is a Magic xpi server thread that constantly checks external systems (such as an email account) to see whether it needs to invoke a flow without waiting for a response. When it needs to invoke a flow, it places a flow message with a status of READY_FOR_USE in the Magic Space.

Each available worker scans the Magic Space for jobs to execute, meaning messages whose status is READY_FOR_USE. When the worker finds a message, it changes the status to IN_PROCESS, passes the message payload to the flow, and executes the flow logic. This is known as a pull mechanism.

*External Triggers.* An external trigger, such as the HTTP Requester or a Web server, is an external application. Once the trigger receives a request, it places a message in the Magic Space that invokes the flow. The synchronous external triggers will also wait for a response message.

2. **Reporting the task as done (polling triggers).** When the main flow is completed, the worker updates the request message's status in the Magic Space to DONE, and is then free to scan for additional messages.

3. **Messaging the Magic Space (external triggers).** If the message is from a synchronic trigger (such as an HTTP trigger), when the flow ends, the worker writes a response message to the Magic Space, which the trigger will send to the client.

4. **Running the Next Parallel Message.** Every parallel and stand-alone branch is also handled as a separate message written by the flow to the Magic Space. This new thread (the parallel or stand-alone branch) can be handled by any of the project's workers, even a worker running on a different machine.

**Magic xpa Application Platform and Magic xpi Integration Platform.** The Magic xpa Application Platform provides a unitary development and deployment framework for multi-channel applications including Mobile, Web, Rich Internet Applications (RIA) and Client Server. Magic xpi Integration Platform and Magic xpa Application Platform together constitute Magic's End-to-End Enterprise Mobility Solution.

Hot Use Case:

Mobile App Integration

*Merit Service Solutions*

Merit Service Solutions used Magic xpi and Magic xpa to deploy a fully integrated mobile app. "We manage approximately 2000 customer sites and wanted a way to take advantage of today's digital and mobile capabilities to streamline processes, and provide the best experience to our customers and our service providers. I am happy to report that Magic's unique solution, combining both mobile and back-end integration under one technology stack, not only provided all the capabilities we demanded, it has also passed the test of an epic blizzard, enabling us to provide our customers with the timely services they expect, even under the most demanding circumstances."

# INDEX

Westmor Industries 71
WSDL 78
xml 84
xsd 84

# ABOUT THE AUTHOR

Glenn Johnson is Senior Vice President of Magic Software Enterprises Americas. Mr. Johnson is the author of the multiple award-winning blog "Integrate My JDE" on ittoolbox.com and contributor to the Business Week Guide to Multimedia Presentations (Osborne-McGraw Hill). He has written on CRM and related topics for CRM Magazine, DestinationCRM.com, customerTHINK, IoT Journal, CMSWire, Enterprise Apps Today, The Enterprisers Project, Data Center Knowledge, Smart Data Collective, World Economic Forum, Inbound Logistics and other publications.

He is the recipient of the Quest International Users Group Partner Distinguished Service Award (2016) and has presented at Collaborate, Interop, COMMON, CIO Logistics Forum and dozens of other user groups and conferences. His interviews on software industry issues have been aired on the NBC Today Show, E! News, Discovery and more.

www.ingramcontent.com/pod-product-compliance
Lightning Source LLC
Chambersburg PA
CBHW071005050326
40689CB00014B/3495